LIVING THE
DREAM

The Story of Lloyd W. "Fig" Newton

To John

Best Wishes for
a great future

Gen fig newton

10-12-21

Aim high —
yes, you can!

B. J. Harvey Hill

D1591047

Lloyd W. "Fig" Newton and B. J. Harvey Hill

ISBN 978-1-64468-454-2 (Paperback)
ISBN 978-1-64468-455-9 (Hardcover)
ISBN 978-1-64468-456-6 (Digital)

Covenant Books, Inc.
11661 Hwy 707
Murrells Inlet, SC 29576
www.covenantbooks.com

Lloyd W. "Fig" Newton

To my entire family, especially to my wife, Elouise M.
Newton, and my parents, John and Annie Newton.

B.J. Harvey Hill

For
RPH, MBH, JPH, ALBH, BSCH
MBH, GHH, BGH,
TYLJ, PBTG,
and LW "F" N

A hometown matters.
It nurtures and guides
As a trellis upon which
Life is entwined.

—B.J. Harvey Hill

CONTENTS

ACKNOWLEDGEMENTS

For the past thirty-one years, my wife Elouise has been right beside me and many times out in front, helping to make critical decisions that shaped our lives. She loved the Air Force and our way of life which made it easy for both of us to serve the nation to the best of our abilities. She was the wind beneath my wings. I also want to thank my parents who shaped and molded me right from the beginning and well into adulthood. I am still in awe of how well they provided for our family with so few resources and difficult barriers they had to endure to survive.

I have often heard that writing about one's self is never an easy task; now I can confirm that statement. This book has been a long time in the making, and I want to thank Mrs. B.J. Harvey Hill for her commitment and hard work to document the story of my life. She was the first to suggest to me that I should consider focusing a book toward younger readers. Immediately, I thought this was a great idea and one I had never considered before. She and her husband, Pat, were very patient and provided excellent advice throughout the process. *Thank you*!

The story of my life is connected to the lives of many people along the way, especially those of the United States Air Force. I want to thank those who were my leaders and those who were led by me. They significantly impacted the development of my leadership skills and my ability to relate to people. There is no question that I am a better person because they came my way. From those caring adults in my community of Ridgeland, South Carolina, to those who supported me at Tennessee State University, and finally to those in the Air Force who taught me so much, *thank you*!

This book describes time, places and events that are recollections of my memories of them. Please appreciate that they are my best knowledge of how and what happened.

—Lloyd W. "Fig" Newton

I first met Lloyd Newton in February 2011 when he was the keynote speaker at Florida Air Museum's Winter Lecture Series. I asked if he had ever considered a book geared toward the younger reader that would tie in with his deep commitment to youth and education. I am very grateful to Gen. Lloyd Newton and Mrs. Elouise Newton for their confidence, their collaboration, and for their story of service.

A long-term goal is rarely accomplished alone. My deep appreciation goes to Matthew B. Hill for his professional counsel and thoughtful, personal encouragement; Judson P. Hill for his personal encouragement and critical commentary; Douglas S. Higgins for historical dimension; my parents and grandparents; Debbi and Karl Kern; Carol Pautler for her USAF Pentagon service; Joseph A. Merluzzi, former Berkeley Preparatory School Headmaster, Tampa, Florida, who challenged professionals and students alike to risk much, reach high, and then stretch a little more. My thanks to M. Joanne Moore; Dr. Cindy Novick; the staff of the Jackson County Public Library, Sylva, North Carolina, for research guidance; Alex Foster, for technical contributions; and the staff of Covenant Publishing, Murrells Inlet, South Carolina. Thanks and apologies for those whose help is not listed here. Finally, thanks to Patrick Hill for his invaluably patient technological support, on-the-spot "fireman" problem-solving abilities and, well, everything!

And I thank you, Reader, for *listening* to the depth of commitment of the man who lived the story.

—B.J. Harvey Hill

Although the authors hope Living the Dream will be of interest to many readers, it was conceived, developed, and written with the young adult reader in mind. Reading is a key in the success of all our lives. We hope this book will be an enjoyable read for all school-age children, especially high school students, and that it will inspire you to complete your high school education and beyond. We believe education is the single most important factor in helping to level the playing field for the success of all people. We want young people to Aim High and Soar to the Stars of Life. With this goal in mind, we dedicate this book to you: young learners everywhere. Enjoy!

—LW"F"N and BJHH

PREFACE

GOPHER HILL

Travel south along South Carolina's Interstate 95. Take either of the two Ridgeland exits just before the Georgia border to reach the county seat of Jasper County. Its original name, Gopher Hill, came from the area's large population of gopher tortoises. This "keystone species" thrived in the upland area's sandy soil, long-leaf pines and turkey oaks.[1]

The name "Gopher Hill" didn't last, though. Later settlers didn't think that was dignified enough for a railroad town—gopher, indeed. So "Ridgeland" was born. The new name was inspired by the regional geography. The area is the Palmetto State's highest point of elevation on its coastal plain and is located between Savannah, Georgia, and Charleston. Today's town is different from the Ridgeland of Lloyd Newton's boyhood in some ways, yet in others it's the same.

On a visit to this near-coastal area, I pulled into a filling station just off the interstate. Two vehicles were parked side by side. One, a made-in-America Chevy, had a "Vietnam Veteran" frame around the rear license plate. The other, a pick-up truck, had a yellow ribbon magnet on the tailgate honoring veterans. Inside I met two of the friendliest strangers on my entire journey. We chatted, laughed, and enjoyed the music playing.

Driving on down the main street, I couldn't miss a huge banner hanging outside a doctor's office. "Character Trait of the Month," it read. I'd never seen anything like that in my town. I drove a few blocks farther, and there he stood! He was in the middle of a small park, perfectly landscaped with annuals and benches. He was a big, beautiful bronze statue of a gopher tortoise, reigning over Gopher Hill Square! Almost as an apology for their ancestors' oversight, the people of Ridgeland have proudly embraced their heritage. Like Aesop, today's Jasper County residences know a good tortoise when they see it. (Any tortoise is a good one!) The Annual Gopher Hill Parade is held the first weekend in October. The Blue Heron Nature Trail provides hikers with a chance to see tortoise burrows year-round.

Ridgeland and Jasper County are the home of *Robert's Rules of Order*, a book containing the internationally accepted method for conducting meetings in an organized, equitable manner. It is also one of the only counties in the country, small as it is, in which two four-star generals in the modern United States military were raised.[2]

The November 9, 2011 copy of the *Jasper County Sun* newspaper ran a front-page story featuring a World War II Navy WAVES (Women Accepted for Volunteer Emergency Service).[3] The Veterans' Day edition honored local residents as an example for others to follow. Service to their country and strength of character are important values to today's Ridgelanders.

—BJHH

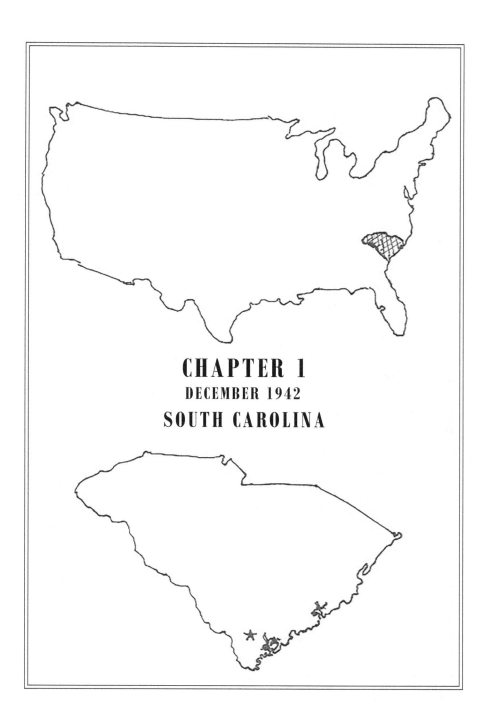

CHAPTER 1
DECEMBER 1942
SOUTH CAROLINA

I t had been a year. America had been at war for a year now. On December 7, 1941, the Japanese had launched a surprise air attack on the United States at Hawaii's Pearl Harbor. President Franklin D. Roosevelt declared war on Japan the next day. A week later, Germany and Italy declared war on America. In a matter of days, the country went from staying neutral to fighting World War II in two theaters— Europe and Asia.

On the first anniversary of the attack, wreckage of sunken ships and planes still blocked parts of Pearl Harbor. Every 1942 newspaper carried headlines of battles in the Pacific and in Europe. Folks living along the southeastern coast of the United States, however, knew that the war was right there at home, too. German U-boats (submarines) had discovered that the coastal shipping industry was still operating at a peacetime level: there were few air patrols, no radio silences, no military escorts for merchant ships, and no light blackouts in coastal cities at night. They boldly sank American merchant marine ships in broad daylight while people on shore watched the smoke and heard the thunder of the explosions on the sinking vessels. The Germans called it "The Great American Hunting Season."

A total of 524 American ships had been sunk off the East Coast between July and December 1942. That was right off the beaches where people were swimming on summer vacation! Yes, a total of 524 ships had gone down in just the last six months![4]

Seven months earlier, the US Coast Guard cutter *Icarus* surprised and sank the German *U-352* off the coast of North Carolina. On May 10, the few German survivors were plucked from the swells. The prisoners of war were delivered to naval and marine personnel at the Charleston Naval Base, South Carolina. They became the first foreign troops to be imprisoned within the United States since the War of 1812.[5]

People in the Carolinas talked about the war in the Pacific and the soldiers over in Europe. But they *definitely* talked about the

German submarines not too many miles offshore. They were especially concerned about just how close the war was getting to their homes. Would they wake up one morning to find German soldiers on their doorsteps? "During the first six months of 1942 residents of North Carolina (and South Carolina) were closer to war than most overseas troops."[6]

Everyone was working for the war effort. Young men and women were volunteering for service. Those still at home did their part by rationing, doing without, and picking up the responsibilities of those who were at war. They were doing a lot of praying, too.

Things were no different in Jasper County, South Carolina. That was home to the Newtons.[7] The family struggled at home, doing their part, while neighbors and family members served. Rural life had never been easy, but the war years were making it tougher on everybody. The naval battles so close to home, rationing of gasoline, food, and other day-to-day items, and lots of little mouths to feed were ever-present worries for John and Annie Newton.

*****

The Plantation was the answer. Yes, Turkey Hill Plantation. Annie Newton was convinced that was where her John needed to be and where he needed to work. A good neighbor and friend, Addie Allen, already worked for the new owner, Jeremiah Milbank. The large commercial farm offered better jobs and benefits when compared to the turpentine-production business where John currently labored. It wasn't any easier or any cooler; neither were the hours any shorter. It offered, however, higher wages, a plantation-owned home, and lots of good acres for both a family garden and cash crops of their own.

Annie hoped these improvements in their lives would increase the chances that this new baby inside her would survive. The woman had already lost two children. Grief and melancholy would wash over her whenever she remembered holding tiny twin Lahar's delicate little hand before he was placed in his coffin just days after he was born or when she thought of their other child who had died before birth.

These sad memories only increased her determination to create a better life for their present and future children in any way she could. So encourage John she did!

Despite the strains of war, the autumn of 1942 was a happy time for the Newton family. John did indeed get that job at Turkey Hill. He liked the work and appreciated the benefits. When Jeremiah Milbank, a New Jersey native, purchased the large tract of Jasper County land, he was determined to use the latest research in agriculture, animal husbandry, and technology to build a *modern* plantation—a profitable and productive business from the soil. Respect for the people, animals, and land would be the key to its success. Now John Newton was helping that plan succeed.

After moving into their new home, Annie continued her daily schedule. Breakfast, gardening, laundry, housework, dinner, and preserving that homegrown food filled her days. Helping with homework, supper, and bedtimes filled the evenings. John, too, worked hard at his job and then into the evening at home and in the community. They were a dedicated team with goals and dreams for their family.

December sped by. Annie knew Christmas preparations had to be completed as much ahead of time as possible. As she cooked, sewed, and created all sorts of good eats and treats, neighbors and family were doing the same. The whole community was abuzz with excitement. Annie couldn't help but notice, though, that her baby's kicking was getting stronger by the day. It wouldn't be long before another Newton arrived to further fill their farmhouse.

John, always concerned about mother and new child, tried to get his precious wife to take it as easy as possible. Slowing her down, however, was about as easy as stopping those crows that snatched a free meal from his cornfields every summer.

Finally, amidst all the little running feet, hungry mouths, and holiday happiness, her body told her it was time. Miss Carrie Johnson, the midwife who had helped bring the other Newton children into the world, was summoned. There were few hospitals for blacks in the 1940s (none in Jasper County) and no black doctors in Ridgeland.

Babies were born at home with experienced midwives handling the birth, the mothers, and the anxious fathers.

This would be sister Dorothy's first time to help Miss Carrie. It would also be the first Newton born in their new home. "I just know I'm getting a baby sister this time," Dottie exclaimed to everybody she met.

John kept the fire going for a warm house and hot water. Dorothy helped by supplying clean cloths and fresh hot water. Mother, baby, and Miss Carrie did their jobs, too. In the early morning hours of Christmas Eve, 1942, the baby was born. John had himself a fifth son, Lloyd Warren Newton, and Dottie was still her daddy's only girl. The newborn's wail was the sweetest carol of the season.

Over the years, Dottie loved to tell Lloyd about how she helped to bring him into the world. (At that early Christmas Eve morning moment, though, Annie was wondering how much of an explorer this little one might be, coming from a town that started out being called Gopher Hill?) Oh my, if she had only known what was in store for her! This baby boy was destined to surprise her!

Present-day plantations are large agricultural centers that grow at least one main crop to be sold—a "cash" crop. These giant farms can be found the world over. The rich alluvial soils of Central America produce cacao and bananas. The mountainsides of certain Hawaiian Islands are covered with pineapple plantations. Tobacco is grown both in the southeastern United States and on large tracts of Caribbean Islands. India exports mango, tea, coffee, and sandalwood. Continental African soils produce cacao, rubber, palm oil, coffee, cotton, tea, and twenty-first century biofuels.[8]

Jeremiah Milbank used the resources of Turkey Hill to concentrate on singular cash crops—predominately southern pines for lumber, long-leaf pines for turpentine, and livestock. He was particularly proud of the crossbred Angus-Hereford, and later Angus-Brahman cattle developed on the plantation. These new breeds could better withstand the heat and eye diseases exacerbated by the tough Carolina climate.[9]

For those days, this was a large, modern agri-business venture that had come to Ridgeland, South Carolina. John Newton would be a valued member of its team for years to come.

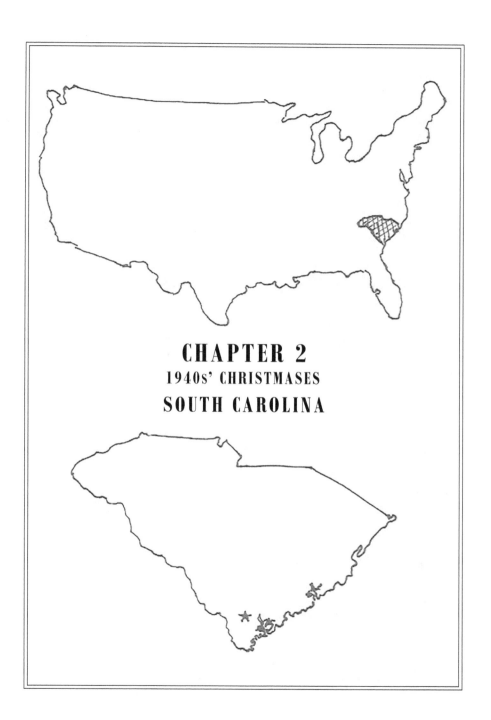

CHAPTER 2
1940s' CHRISTMASES
SOUTH CAROLINA

The Newton Turkey Hill farmhouse was filled with lots of love and lots of little Newtons! Lloyd raced to keep up with his older brothers as they ran through the loblolly pines and hayfields of Jasper County. He'd hug his big sister, Dottie, as she whispered just the right word for a baby brother's tears. Before too long, though, he was no longer the baby. Two more boys joined the Newton clan. Yes, two more boys. Dorothy was destined to remain Daddy's only little girl.

John and Annie's children were: Herman, the eldest, Dorothy, James, an infant lost before birth, Lamar, his twin Lahar, who died in infancy, Marion, Lloyd, Lester, and Donald. The lack of good medical care took the lives of many children during the first half of the twentieth century—black and white, rich and poor. Lahar died of jaundice, a common malady of newborns that is easily treated in the pediatric wings of hospitals today. Eight of Annie and John's ten babies made it to adulthood, remaining a close family still to the present.

Christmas was a special time. John and Mr. Otto Shaw, a close friend and Turkey Hill coworker, were responsible for the highlight of the neighborhood celebration—the annual barbeque pig roast for the Christmas church program. It began with the pit, a big hole dug out away from the house over by the sugar cane mill. Inside this covered mill-shed with its wide door was a big black kettle. It was used for cooking sugar cane into molasses around Thanksgiving. Now the shed would be used as cover for preparing the sauces and other fixings that would be "mopped" on the hogs during the roast. Two "secret" recipes that included Heinz 57, Worchester sauce, pepper, and lots of vinegar made little mouths water as they awaited the feast. One sauce was for basting and the other for eating. The cane mill shed was a gathering spot throughout the year for any number of jobs. An awful lot of good memories came from that spot on the farm.

The pigs would be roasting for many hours, beginning at about four o'clock on Christmas Eve morning. A goodly supply of oak was needed for cooking with big coals to create that full flavor. John and Otto kept a lookout for just the right kind of wood throughout the fall so the cutting, toting, and stacking would be completed ahead of time. The mules would pull the logs into place in the days leading up to the cooking.

Setting up the barbeque was serious business. The pit needed to be eighteen to twenty-four inches deep and of adequate width to accommodate more than one whole hog. After the hogs were butchered, long metal rods were inserted into the meat through the hips and the shoulders. The ends of these rods would be laid on a board along the edge of the pit, suspending the pigs over the deep pit full of smoldering coals. One side would roast nice and slow for a good, long while, with very close supervision and lots of sauce "mopping" to ensure the tender juiciness. Every few hours, a couple of strong men would lift the rods, carefully turn the hogs, and settle them down for the other side to roast. Spreading the coals and tending the fire were all important for temperature control and even cooking.

The decorations on the Christmas tree out in the yard, the smoke from the barbeque pit snaking its way skyward, and the sweet smell of basted meat would increase the excitement of the day close to torture level. Happy feet, perfect behavior (or at least the attempt), and helpful hands added to the holiday joy. The camaraderie of the menfolk around the roasting pit was as satisfying as that first taste of juicy, smoky pork dripping down a chin. When the meat was finally ready and all the stomachs were growling with hunger, everyone would clean up, dress up, and head to church where the meal was served after the evening service and the children's program.

Church began with the children performing their well-practiced rendition of the Christmas Story. Over the years, all the Newton children participated in this important holiday tradition. The big smiles on lots of squirmy little children revealed their excitement over what came next. The Milbanks sent gifts and food to the church families, and Santa would always arrive with a big bag of gifts. Lloyd looked forward to the huge candy cane *and* the $1.00 which every good little boy and girl received. To be honest, though, he was really looking forward to turning ten. That's when the *big* boys and girls were given $5.00!

These gifts of cash were very generous for that time. Minimum wage was 30 cents per hour. Milk cost 60 cents per gallon and gasoline was 19 cents per gallon[10] Yes, the youngsters' $1.00 meant a lot to them, however, the $5.00 gift for the older children was very important. One dollar in 1945, when Lloyd was three, was worth $12.16 in 2014 dollars.[11] That $5.00 "Abraham Lincoln" would buy something pretty special! It also provided a lesson in saving and spending wisely.

After church and that delicious barbeque meal, for some reason, every single child was suddenly very sleepy and needed to go right home to bed—the only night of the year *that* ever happened! Before bed, however, each little Newton would scout out their special place around the house to set their hats in which Santa would place each child's gifts. Then one last glance out that window by the chimney where their "prettiest Christmas tree ever" was standing in the yard, and then it was rush, rush, rush, jump into bed, and cover their heads! What an incredible birthday Lloyd had—every single Christmas Eve! Lloyd never minded having to share his birthday with that holiday; he always thought this day was special just for him and the Lord!

Each Christmas morning, the children would awaken early (of course) and run through the house to *their* hats. Being the good, hard-working children they were, Santa had been sure to find where every single one had been set. "My hat! My hat! *Wow!* Look at my hat!" they would call to one another. They were always stuffed with an apple, orange, and tangerines. Next, they hurriedly tore into those special gifts. The pops and snaps of firecrackers and new cap pistols replaced the quiet morning stillness, awakening Mom and Dad from their gift of a little bit more sleep once a year.

"Mommy, Mommy, look what Santa brought me," someone would shout.

"Yes, Child. Yes, Child" was Annie's soft reply.

Another treasured Christmas treat came from their family friend, Addie Allen. She had the only fig tree around in the area. Each season she would share this favorite fruit of Lloyd's as her gift to their family. Christmas morning was all the more memorable to the children because, like many families across America, they didn't get a lot of extra things in between holidays. But oh, what memories those Christmas mornings gave them all!

(Author's Note: Hearing Lloyd W. Newton recount this story with infectious excitement and joy was just like being there on that South Carolina plantation with him and his family!—BJHH)

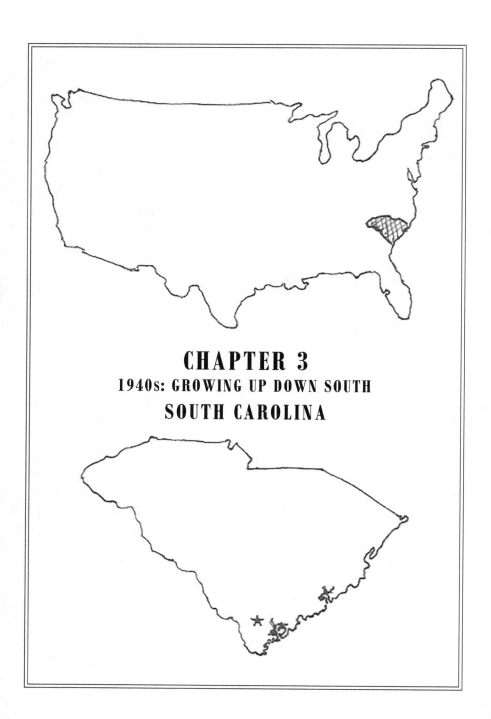

CHAPTER 3
1940s: GROWING UP DOWN SOUTH
SOUTH CAROLINA

Being a country boy could be fun when there was time. It wasn't always easy, that's for sure, but everybody pitched in. Each child had a specific chore. Lloyd's was providing wood for the kitchen stove while his closest older brother, Marion, would bring in the wood for the fireplace. Together they carried many a cord into the house.

Ridgeland's Atlantic Coastal Plain, an ancient ocean floor, was covered for millennia with mire and ooze. Modern land management techniques were gradually making it more productive. That didn't mean that farm work was any easier. The Newtons worked their garden located beside a creek about a quarter mile down the road past the sugar cane shed. The lower ground there held more moisture on a consistent basis, which was important in the Carolina heat. The family also worked several fifteen-to-twenty-acre parcels of Turkey Hill farmland for their cash crops of feed corn, beans, and cotton.

Planting a spring garden, a winter garden, and field crops meant they had plenty of vegetables to "put up" (to can and preserve for the winter). The preserved food would be carefully stacked in the storehouse out back of their house. When the children would open the door to that cool, dark shed, it took a moment for their eyes to adjust to the low light inside. Then their gaze would gradually pick out row after row of the family's hard work. Waiting in front of them, as colorful as a carefully stitched calico quilt, were jars of tomatoes, okra, butter beans, snap beans, and snap peas. Weighing down the shelves beside those sat more jars filled with peaches and pears from the neighbors' trees. Sweet potatoes, ready for baking, lay in teepee-shaped potato banks. The family also raised hogs, cows, and chickens for meat. Lloyd grew up, like most black farm kids back then, knowing how to make flour and meal from corn and molasses from sugar cane.

Everyday Annie and the children would head out, tools in hand, to chop (hoe) the cotton and other crops. She would stay right beside them in the field, giving instructions on how to handle the horses and mules. John would join them after his job at the plantation was over. Before dark, the animals were brought in and fed. Supper followed, usually with John still out in the field. Annie created delicious meals from the harvest wrestled from that stubborn southern soil. How satisfying it was to sit down at the table knowing they had grown that plateful all by themselves!

The children did their homework by the light of kerosene lamps. Lloyd vividly remembers his fourth-grade year, around 1950 or '51. Jeremiah Milbank brought electricity to Turkey Hill and to the houses of his workers. The young boy would always remember when that lone electric light bulb hanging from the living room ceiling "popped on." It was truly a new day for the Newton family. They may not have been any less tired at homework time, but they now had much better light in which to finish it.

Lloyd calls his mother a great "CEO" (Chief Executive Officer, otherwise known as "The Boss") as she managed her children, resources, and responsibilities. Perhaps "CEM" for Chief Executive Mom would have been another good title for her. She was good at helping her children learn to work together. These lessons were just the beginning of Lloyd's leadership training. As soon as he could walk, he remembers wanting to be out there with his father, his big brothers, and his mother. "Lloyd, bring me some of that water so I can put it on these tomatoes," she would ask her little boy, giving him a job that was needed and one that he could manage on his own.

"Practice makes perfect." John would admonish his charges. The Newton boys learned that lesson well as they plowed their sandy farmland. They would plow, then Daddy would check their work… uh-oh. Those rows weren't quite straight enough, so they plowed them again. Then Daddy checked again…still not quite straight enough, so more plowing. The boys ended up with some mighty fine *straight* rows of corn in those Jasper County fields.

Lloyd remembers John's lesson "straight" from his heart. "Hard work doesn't hurt anybody. It builds strength of body, mind and purpose." Yes, Herman, Dorothy, James, Lamar, Marion, Lloyd, Lester, and Donald developed valuable character traits thanks to their parents.

Lloyd didn't think about it, but the world of his childhood was not the same as it had been when his parents were growing up. The sky was different now. Every now and then, droning sounds would drift across the clouds in the distance. All the kids would stop and look up or run out of the house hoping they didn't miss it. Then as the sounds grew closer, they would squint into the sun to see airplanes and Zeppelins! The plane might be an open-cockpit bi-wing crop duster treating hundreds of acres of surrounding farmland. It might be a commercial DC-3,[12] carrying people to faraway places. Or it might be the military training planes he admired so much. If it was one of the rigid Zeppelin airships droning slowly overhead, the children would stand for long minutes watching the airshow in the low-country sky. Yes, the sky *was* different from that of his parents' childhood and how Lloyd loved it!

Living in southern South Carolina during the 1940s and 1950s meant seeing a lot of young people, mostly men, in military uniform. The Newtons were near the Marines' Parris Island basic training facility, Hunter Army Airfield near Savannah, Georgia, and Charleston Naval Base. Often, his father would offer rides to young soldiers, sailors, and marines. Lloyd hung onto every word as they spoke of the War and their service. His cousin, Lee Newton, a soldier in the Army, would stop by the house when he was home on leave. The boy noticed how straight he stood; how important he looked each time he walked through the door in his uniform. The young boy liked the look of those shined shoes, crisply pressed shirts and slacks, correct posture, and tilted cap. He also respected what they represented. Members of Lee Newton's generation were serving their country. Lloyd decided he would be part of the next generation to do so.

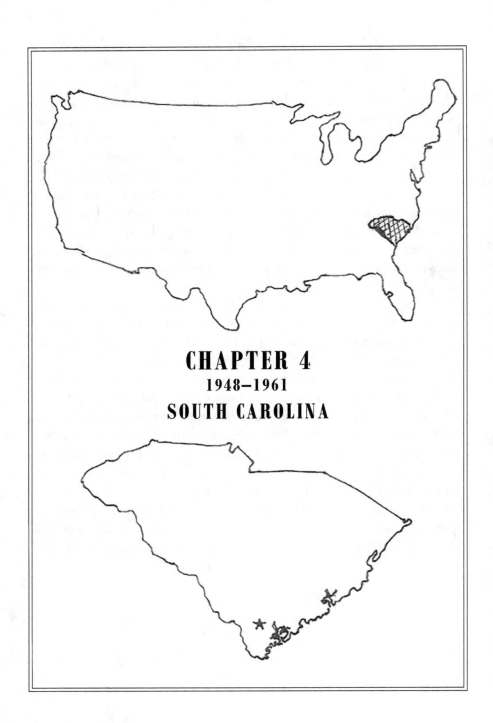

CHAPTER 4
1948–1961
SOUTH CAROLINA

Jasper County's population was small, so naturally the schools were also small. From first grade through sixth, the Newton children attended Gillisonville Elementary, a four-room building for all the black children of the area. Yes, just the black children. This was a time of segregation in the United States. African-Americans were legally bound as to where they could or could not go and what they could or could not do just because of the color of their skin. Black and white children went to separate schools. It was a dreadful and unjust time. Many years later, Dr. Martin Luther King Jr. and many other brave Americans of all races would stand up to change this. In the 1940s, however, that was the way it was for Lloyd and his family. "Do everything you do to the best of your ability," his father had taught him. So, segregation or not, Lloyd worked hard in school. He found that he was pretty good at it, too.

John and Annie had limited educational opportunities when they were young. John only went to school through second grade, while Annie had to withdraw after sixth grade. Their families needed them at home. They had both loved the classroom, the books, and most of all, the learning! As they met and planned their life together, they set a goal for their future children. It was an ambitious, world-changing goal—all of their children would graduate from high school! At a time when most poor black people seldom had the chance to finish even elementary school, this was a bold idea, but the couple knew education was important and that it changed lives.

Many decades later, Lloyd's wife, Elouise, would make an observation about her father-in-law: "That man knew how important a good education would be for his children," she recalled. "Dad just knew stuff. If he had had a formal education, he would have been like an Einstein."

Even before Lloyd went to first grade, he had learned something about school from his older brothers and sister. Everyone was expected to really behave themselves! Getting in trouble at school meant getting in trouble all over again at home. The black teachers with their college educations and wealth of knowledge were true success stories. They were to be obeyed. From the first day of school, Lloyd respected and feared the women and men at the front of those classrooms. Once he got to know them, though, he saw that they were working as hard as he was, both at school and at home. Many of them farmed like his family did.

During his fifth-grade year, Providence shined down on the Newton family. Dorothy, then living and working in New York City, sent $430 home to her parents. This enabled them to purchase their own farm. It was now *Newton* land on which crops could be grown and sold to raise money for their needs. *(Note: Today it remains the Newton farm for all the family to enjoy.)*

A family can try its hardest and work its longest, yet conversely, no one is immune from hardships. John and Annie had lost two children as infants. They had endured racism. They had battled poverty. Still, their children thrived. In 1949, when Lloyd was in grade school, Tragedy, that ever-present condition lurking at the edge of human experience, rose up again. Lloyd's eldest brother, Herman, left South Carolina in search of a better life in the Northeast. One day in Brooklyn, New York, however, that quest ended when he was shot and killed by a Brooklyn policeman. John and Annie now had two babies and their firstborn gone. Although their faith gave the promise of a future reunion, the loss of these siblings remained a tender subject to everyone in the close-knit Newton family.

Junior High and High School

Rural South Carolina may have been small-town in nature, but it was not closed to the rest of the world. Newspapers, radio, magazines, books, and later, television told of different cultures and opportunities. John and Annie's long-term goal was being realized. One by one, their children were succeeding in school and graduating from Jasper County High School. Dorothy had moved to New York

City with Aunt Elizabeth where the jobs were more plentiful, the pay was better, and life for African-Americans was more palpable. Some of her brothers joined her later.

A great migration of black Americans had begun following the Civil War in the mid-1860s and continued into the twentieth century. People were leaving the farms of the South for Northeastern and Midwestern factory jobs.[13] Other nationalities were doing the same, emigrating from farms in the Midwest or European homelands, turning America into an industrial nation. For African-Americans, though, they were also hoping to leave behind racial segregation for the more open culture of northern cities. Discrimination was there, too, but not to the same extent. Change was still needed throughout America. It would come; slowly, surely, it would come.

A teenaged Lloyd was still committed to his long-ago goal of following in his cousin's footsteps. Lee Newton had become one of *the first six Sergeant Majors in modern US Army history*, but he chose not to explain this to anybody in his family until years later after he retired. They just knew he was "Sergeant Major Newton." Lloyd was growing up in a family dedicated to serving their country to the best of their ability.

Lloyd's high school years were speeding by. Serving his community presented him with another job opportunity. Imagine today's high school students stepping onto the school bus the first day of school to find one of their friends in the driver's seat. That's exactly where Lloyd found himself during his junior and senior years—driving a Jasper County school bus. He carried fifty to sixty children to school every day and got them there safely and on time.

He was only 16 years old, yet he was already envisioning his future. While riding horses with his brothers or his good friend and cousin, Joe Ferguson, he would bend their ears about his plans. Certain specifics he had already decided: he wanted a military career, and he wanted to leave home. Like so many young people throughout history, he wanted to get away on his own to a place where nobody knew him, where he could have a fresh start.

The summers leading into his junior and senior years were spent with family but not in Jasper County. Big brothers Marion and Lamar, sister Dorothy, and Annie's baby sister, Aunt Sarah, were now living and working in Boston. Those bus rides from South Carolina to Massachusetts and the months spent in that historic city opened his eyes to America's geography and her past. During his first Boston summer, he worked in the "Walk by Charles" dress factory. Prior to his senior year, he worked with a maintenance company cleaning offices and hospitals. More jobs meant more savings for his post-high-school-graduation plans.

One fall day during his senior year at JHS, he was told to go to the school library for a meeting. There he found several of his classmates gathered around, chatting with a military recruiter who, at that time, represented the US Air Force. The recruiter gave his "pitch" and convinced the boys that Air Force life was for them. This new branch of the military services presented an exciting opportunity for these high school boys. In fact, the group decided Lloyd would be their troop leader when they reached boot camp. That's how quickly they became committed. The man explained he would return in a few weeks to administer the entrance exams, and they would be off to the Air Force following graduation.

Within a few days of that meeting, one of Lloyd's teachers, Mr. Fouch Shanklin, pulled him aside during recess.

"What's this I hear about you going into the military?" Shanklin asked.

"Yes," Lloyd responded with excitement in his voice. "We're going into the Air Force."

"I thought you would be going to college. You have a good head on your shoulders, you know. I think you could be a mechanical engineer. Plus, if you go to college, you can still go into the military."

Shanklin went on to explain that a future officer required a degree. Lloyd didn't know what a mechanical engineer did nor did he fully understand the officer rank, but he was surprised by his teacher's interest in his welfare. This was the first time anyone had talked seriously to Lloyd about going to college. He could have a degree *and* a uniform!

As the school year continued, military and college talk peppered his conversations. Having both family and work experience in Boston, he began investigating the College of Engineering at Northeastern University. Its work-study program enabled students to pay for their education by ten-week rotations of academic classes and engineering jobs. Upon graduation, the new engineers would have both a degree and valuable work experience. Boston would also be a place where he could live with family. He would not, however, be in a place where no one knew him.

One day, he and good friend/musician Harry James Frazier were in the band room, bantering back and forth about which college would be the best to attend. Harry James had not been at that library meeting with the Air Force recruiter. His dreams centered on college and a university marching band. He had studied and practiced music with that vision in mind.

The band director overheard their conversation and walked over. "Did I hear the two of you discussing which college would be the best to attend?"

"Yes, Sir."

"Well," he continued, "the *only* school to go to is Tennessee A & I (Agriculture and Industrial) State University in Nashville, Tennessee. (Today it is known as Tennessee State University, a renowned historically-black university with distinguished alumni throughout the country and the world, including Olympian Wilma Rudolph, Ralph Boston, and Oprah Winfrey.[14]) It has the best band anywhere in the country, and there are lots of pretty girls down the street at Fisk University!" This Tennessee A & I alumnus definitely knew how to get high school boys' attention! He was proud to recommend his alma mater to these two energetic and talented low-country young men.

Lloyd and Harry just sat there a moment without saying anything.

Then Lloyd asked, "Where did you say it is?"

"Nashville, Tennessee," he repeated.

The only two things Lloyd knew about Nashville were Randy's Record Shop and WLAC, the radio station that broadcast its great music all over the Southeast, filling his high school nights with energy and soul. Neither young man had ever been to Tennessee, but suddenly a plan came together. This was a great idea! "This is someplace we can go where no one knows us. It will be just the two of us doing what we want, and we will be away from Jasper County."

Lloyd's teachers, like his parents, challenged him to "take life where it was" and make the best of it. Segregation was a hurdle. It wasn't an excuse to limit life's dreams. No matter the challenge, setting goals and making *good* decisions were what would dictate his future. Bowing to adversity was not part of his plan. "Circumstances do not define one's destiny, your decisions define your destiny," he would later say.

College? John and Annie's big dream was to have all their children graduate from high school. *College?* they thought. Yes, John and Annie, college indeed!

In later years, Newton would reflect on the crucial timing of those two conversations. What if Mr. Shanklin had never pulled him aside in that recess yard? What if he had never brought up the recruiter's visit or questioned Lloyd's enlistment plans? How did he even find out about the meeting? Lloyd had certainly never discussed it with him. Yet here was a teacher who had taken an active interest in a young man, enough so that he kept track of what Lloyd was up to. He saw both youthful potential and a need for guidance. And what if that high school band director had not shared the information about his well-respected alma mater?

Fouch Shanklin was much more aware than his young students were of the world into which these early 1960s graduates were about to enter. The United States was entrenched in the Cold War and was becoming increasingly involved in the conflict between North and South Vietnam. He watched as more and more young men without college deferments were drafted and sent to those Southeast Asian jungles to fight. He knew the risks, especially for poor young black men. He was saddened by the losses of young American potential, dreams, and lives.

Lloyd Newton has never lost his deep appreciation for these two teachers. He shutters whenever he dares to think, *What if they hadn't cared?* Or what if he hadn't heeded their advice?

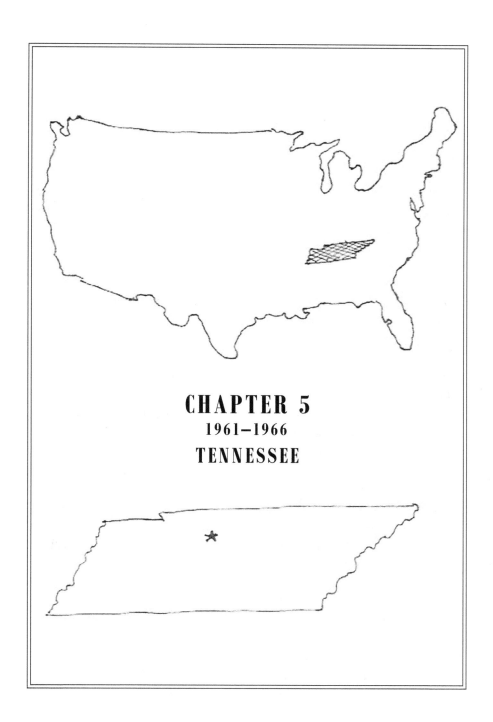

CHAPTER 5
1961–1966
TENNESSEE

*T*ennessee State University, founded in 1912, is located in Nashville, Tennessee, 522 miles from South Carolina's Low Country. The city is the second largest in the state, unlike the rural countryside Lloyd was leaving. The population of Ridgeland in 2000 was 2,518. When Lloyd arrived on campus in 1961, the TSU campus had more people than his home county. Lloyd felt right at home, though, when he read the university's motto: "Enter to learn; go forth to serve."[15] That sure sounded a lot like Momma and Daddy.

Although Lloyd had worked many different jobs for years, he still didn't have enough money for college. So off he headed to Boston to work one more summer to shore up his finances. Finally, in August of 1961, the day arrived for that long-anticipated bus ride across the Appalachian spine of the eastern United States to the capital of Tennessee. The TSU campus, three-and-a-half miles west of downtown Nashville, was his fresh start.

Freshman orientation encouraged the students' involvement in extracurricular activities. Long-time friend Harry James Frazer and Lloyd again found themselves in a large room trying to make decisions about their future. Harry James was selected as a member of the TSU marching band, and Lloyd signed up for the Air Force Drill Team, the "Tiger Jets," featuring a uniform of crisp pleats, a white belt with a big chrome buckle, and a chrome helmet. These activities would provide many memories for these two friends, including football game performances and travel to the away games. Later, an exceptional honor was afforded the TSU Air Force Drill Team during the year Lloyd served as Drill Team Commander. In January 1965, they were invited to Washington, DC to participate in President Lyndon B. Johnson's inaugural parade. Relishing the experience of the nation's capital, he wondered if he would ever return.

When the time came for the two young friends to choose their major courses of study, Harry James and Lloyd encouraged each other once again. Being close enough to teasingly tell others that they were "half-brothers," they stuck together once again, heading into aviation. Harry James had already decided to become a pilot, so he selected Aviation Education as his major. Lloyd leaned toward mechanical engineering, which his high school teacher had recommended. It took only two academic quarters and some tough engineering courses, however, to change his mind. He too selected Aviation Education and immediately saw a big difference in his grades. Cs became B+s. This detour taught him "when you find something you really love, you'll be good at it. Often, the choosing in life is the tough part."

For a long time, Lloyd had been thinking of his cousin, Sergeant Major Lee Newton, and that Army uniform. Becoming a TSU Tiger threw a curve into that plan. The high school military recruiter and the TSU ROTC (Reserved Officers Training Corps) were Air Force, not Army. What was different about the Air Force? Airplanes! The little boy who used to run outside to look up into the sky was now a young man about to become part of that sky. Another new uniform hung in the closet: an ROTC flight suit.

Serving in ROTC introduced Lloyd to a new level of mentors—military-trained and disciplined. Drill Team advisor, Captain Robert T. Dickerson, a fighter pilot, helped Newton throughout his TSU career, especially later with Lloyd's responsibilities as the team's commander. Newton's friendship with Bob Dickerson extended into his Air Force active-duty years and continues today. He learned a valuable lesson early in life—keeping in touch with family, friends, and mentors does take time and effort. But the rewards reaped from these lasting relationships are invaluable.

Two members of the renowned Tuskegee Airmen were also on the ROTC faculty. Both Howard Lee Baugh, and later, Hannibal M. Cox Jr. were part of the World War II Army Air Corps Tuskegee Experiment, which for the first time in history, trained African-American pilots. These men then joined the war effort, flying P-51 Mustangs emblazoned with their signature Red Tails, and provided fighter cover for bombers over enemy territory in Europe. The Tuskegee squadron never lost a single bomber! Following the war and after several other assignments, both Baugh and Cox had accepted positions in the Tennessee State ROTC department.

Newton learned a valuable leadership lesson about inclusion from these men. When the Tuskegee Experiment was formed (named after its location in Tuskegee, Alabama), all the African-Americans involved in the training and maintenance of these aircraft: pilots, navigators, bombardiers, maintenance and support staff were called "Tuskegee Airmen." Acknowledgement of and respect for the entire team, not just the pilots, built a cohesiveness that contributed to the success of this Experiment.[16] Lloyd had the good fortune to spend up-close-and-personal time with both of these American heroes throughout his college career. Baugh was Newton's original ROTC Detachment Commander. Cox followed Baugh and was the officer who commissioned Newton upon graduation. Newton still feels today that receiving his Air Force commission from a member of the historic Tuskegee Airmen was one of the highest honors he could have been given.

Lloyd's TSU days were full. There were the classes, the studying, and yes, there was the partying. Howard Baugh, Jr., the Detachment Commander's son, and Lloyd became close friends, spending lots of good times together.

One day, Howard turned to his buddy and spontaneously called, "Hey, Fig! Fig Newton!"

Lloyd slowly turned toward him with a grin. Guys standing around glanced at each other, thinking, *That sounds pretty good.*

After TSU, while the two friends were in flight school together, Howard continued to call Lloyd "Fig" Newton and introduced him as "Fig" to the other student pilots. Later on, when he was serving overseas in Vietnam, his flight-suit name patch read, "Fig Newton." From that day to this, Fig Newton it has been.

Lloyd was able to afford the Tennessee State tuition and expenses because of two things—the school's work-study programs during the academic year and his return trips to Boston for summer and holiday part-time work. Newton is forever grateful to Mr. Sullivan at downtown Boston's Gilchrist Department Store who, knowing Lloyd's financial needs and service goals, always found a job opening for him.

Both Fig's life and America's were changing in the early 1960s. Throughout history, change has not been easily accomplished without hard work and sacrifice. The college man and the nation both experienced this. Just a few hundred miles south of Nashville, in Atlanta, Georgia, a young black minister, Dr. Martin Luther King Jr. and his followers throughout the country began an historic campaign for civil rights and an end to segregation. The summer of 1963 was a crucial one for America and the civil rights movement. A nationwide call had gone out for a peaceful demonstration march (peaceful, yet risky) to be held on August 23 on the Mall in Washington, DC.

Knowing that his college-student employee was scheduled to work that day, Fig's Gilchrist supervisor, Mr. Sullivan, asked, "Newton, do you want to go?" *Yes*, he did want to go, but he chose not to make the trip because he needed to save his money for college. His boss's kindness, however, was an example of how many Americans of all ages, ethnic groups, and backgrounds showed support for young future leaders during this historic time.

The nation's involvement in the war in Southeast Asia against North Vietnam and in support of South Vietnam's efforts for independence continued. It was a controversial conflict. Americans were asking themselves and their leaders: should the United States be involved? Should our troops be there? As Lloyd thought about his future in the Air Force, he and his classmates often discussed their military and civilian responsibilities. Where could Fig best serve his nation—with the armed forces, with the civil rights movement, in some other capacity? These were difficult choices for the young cadet. Future events and decisions would shape that choice.

In the fall of 1964, Newton was in the middle of his TSU academic career. He was looking forward to checking out an Air Force aerial demonstration team performing that weekend at Sewart Air Force Base (AFB) in Smyrna, Tennessee. It sounded pretty interesting! As soon as Fig saw the F-100 Super Sabres fighter jets in their red, white, and blue Thunderbird paint schemes, heard the engines roar, and watched the tight formations race across the skies, he was spellbound. He was awestruck. He was hooked! Somehow, some way, someday, he decided then and there, he *must* join the USAF Thunderbirds. He didn't know at the time, however, that no black pilot had ever been a member of the Thunderbird team. He just knew he was willing to go for it.

About this time in his college career, during a visit home, Fig's father asked him and his brothers a question: "What's the most important four-letter word in the dictionary: _ _ _ _?"

The boys started guessing: "Is it *love*? Is it *work*?" Even after pooling all their ideas, they couldn't come up with the right answer.

Mr. Newton slowly and dramatically spelled: K-N-O-W. Yes, knowledge—*know*ledge was the most important thing! John believed the more his sons knew, the better off they were going to be. Get knowledge and then put it to work. The brothers certainly knew about work!

Being a TSU Tiger was a *big* plus in Lloyd's life. He had wonderful campus experiences that he could not even have imagined before his arrival. He made a promise to himself to make the most of every one of those experiences, to "be where he was; to be in the moment" rather than to think about what was in the past or what was to come. He put his dad's advice to good use right away—K-N-O-W indeed!

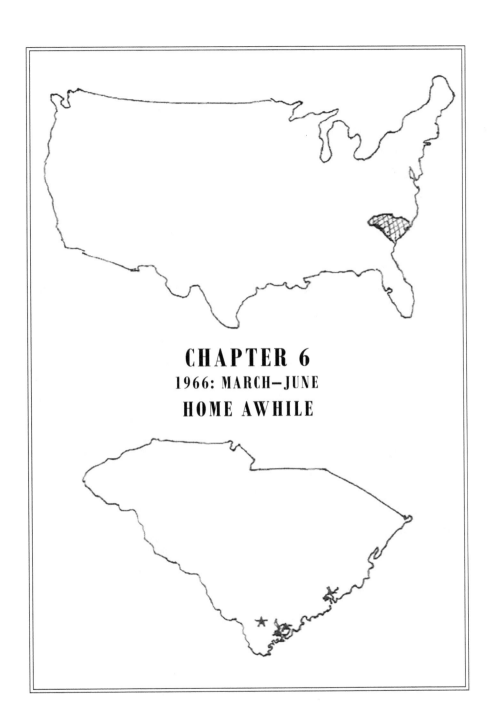

CHAPTER 6
1966: MARCH–JUNE
HOME AWHILE

Graduating from TSU in March of 1966 with his Bachelor of Science degree in Aviation Education and his Air Force military commission, Fig said goodbye to the Tigers and hello to the USAF. Along with his diploma, he had had the honor of being commissioned into the US Air Force by Colonel Hannibal Cox, veteran World War II Tuskegee Airman.

Before leaving Tennessee, however, Lloyd exercised his new status as a commissioned active-duty serviceman. He contacted Broadway National Bank in San Antonio, Texas that did a lot of business with the military. At the time, it was offering a special financing promotion. Fig answered some questions, filled out some paperwork, and he was all set. He watched the Nashville skyline fall away in the rearview mirror of his brand-new, light blue 1966 Pontiac LeMans. He couldn't wait to drive into Ridgeland in that!

The second lieutenant headed home for a short vacation before reporting for active duty in June. "I wanted to hurry up and get my degree and then get my commission and then get into flight school. I couldn't do it fast enough," reflects Fig today.

His time spent in Jasper County was glorious. John and Annie had their son back for a little while. John had a new set of wheels of his own—a new tractor. How he smiled watching his college-graduate son working that new machine in the Newton field! Fig put in three good solid months of work with that tractor, while also enjoying great times with his family, friends, and that new car.

Two weeks before heading to Williams AFB near Phoenix, Arizona, Fig decided on a LeMans road trip to Boston. Brothers Lester, another Newton TSU student, and Donald, still at Jasper High School, along with niece Karen and cousin Joanne, joined him. They planned to leave late at night (after one last evening out with friends) and drive straight through from South Carolina to Massachusetts. Lester took the first shift, driving from midnight to around four o'clock. Then Fig took the wheel. About forty-five minutes later, in the early-morning darkness, he fell asleep. The next thing he knew was that he had crashed his vehicle into the rear of a car on I-95 between Smithfield and Benson, North Carolina. His brand-new, light blue 1966 Pontiac LeMans didn't look so good then!

A shaken and frightened Lloyd couldn't believe what he had just done! The first and most important thing was to make sure no one was hurt. Remarkably, everyone was fine. With that good news established, Fig's emotions crashed. He remembers: "The boo-hoo-ing started as I saw my brand-new Pontiac *and* my whole Air Force career going down the drain."

As the group of young black people gave thanks for everyone's safety, the circumstances of their situation settled around them. This was the 1960s. The efforts of Dr. Martin Luther King Jr. and his supporters to replace racial injustices and prejudices with equality and harmony had often resulted, instead, in confusion and conflicts. They were alone and away from home. They were stranded on a highway in the dark of a North Carolina night. How would this play out? As cars traveling north slowed down to get a better look, one driver asked, "Do you want me to call the police?"

Fig answered with a big, "*Yes!*" as he wiped the tears from his face.

A North Carolina Highway Patrol car arrived. It pulled onto the shoulder of the road, leaving the lights flashing. A white, male officer whose name badge read "Patrolman King," walked over to the shaken group, all the while taking a survey of the accident site. He asked if anyone was hurt. With the answer being "No," he walked the drivers of the two vehicles over to his squad car and asked them to get inside. He was writing up the report while holding Fig's driver's license in his hand when he said, "Newton, tell me what happened."

Lloyd was nervous. He had already tried to come up with some type of story to make this sound good. But nothing he could think of worked. He decided the best approach was to tell the truth and tell his story straight up, just like it happened. "I saw the car. Then I passed out. When I woke up, the car was right in front of me. I tried to miss him, but I didn't make it."

The other driver gave the same account of the event.

"Okay," Patrolman King said calmly, "we've got to go back to the sheriff's department in the nearest town, which is Benson."

Fig stayed with him in the Dodge patrol car while the other driver got out. Even though still upset, he was very impressed when the officer changed gears and that powerful engine took off. (Oh, how men do love their machines!)

Walking into the station, they saw the county sheriff sitting behind the counter with his feet up on the desk having an early-morning cup of coffee. "Good morning, King. What can I do for you?"

"Good morning, Sheriff," the state trooper began. "Mr. Newton had a little problem out on the highway."

"What's the problem?" the sheriff asked.

The trooper continued, "He failed to pass two feet to the left of the car in front of him, and he would like to know how he could take care of this."

Was Fig hearing this correctly? "Failed to pass two feet to the left?" How can he take care of this? Offering help in getting him back on the road? No mention of the word *accident*? Calling him "Mr." Newton? *This is 1966, and we are in North Carolina*, he thought. Yet, Fig had heard it right, "*Mr.* Newton."

The two officers held a brief conference. They decided that Fig had to sign an affidavit stating he was guilty and pay $21.50 to cover court costs for the "illegal passing" traffic fine. The word *guilty* caught Fig's attention. He just knew he was going to a North Carolina jail. Then he heard the rest of the story: pay $21.50, and he could go on his way. He couldn't get his wallet out of his pocket fast enough!

Patrolman King then took Fig back to the scene, put everyone in his patrol car, and used that powerful Dodge to transport the family to Smithfield's Pontiac dealership. He also called for a tow truck to pull the damaged LeMans to the dealership for repairs. Since the other vehicle was not badly damaged and could still be driven, that driver was released to proceed on his way. (The Newton family has always been thankful for this stranger. While Fig was at the sheriff's office, the other driver had remained at the accident scene with the remaining young people to ensure their safety and to help to settle their nerves.) After an unsuccessful and heated discussion between the state trooper and the dealership regarding getting Fig another car, Patrolman King dropped Fig and his family off at the bus station where they purchased tickets to Raleigh. There, he told them, was the closest rental car location.

That North Carolina Highway Patrolman had taken care of the Newton family that night as carefully as John Newton would have. In getting to know each other during their back-and-forth car trips, King learned that Fig was headed for active duty in a very few days. They both understood that probably meant Vietnam. Fig learned that King's brother had already paid the ultimate sacrifice over there. In an instant, a lasting bond was welded between these two men. In a time of much civil unrest, Patrolman King was one of the candles that would help light the way to a brighter future. This "bad" experience was a turning point for Fig in his attitude toward law enforcement. This Southern white man, this Carolina officer, unknowingly helped to heal some of the lingering hurt from that New York policeman's actions of long ago when he had killed Fig's brother, Herman. Fig has carried Patrolman King's kindness with him throughout the decades of his life. His only regret today is never finding King again. Tragedy is colorblind. Why should Peace not be the same?

After a shorter-than-planned Boston visit and with the Pontiac out of service, Fig had ten days to get from New England to Arizona. Late on a Monday evening, he climbed aboard a Greyhound coach. North Carolina, Georgia, South Carolina, Alabama, Mississippi. The further the bus's circuitous route took him from his friends and family, the sadder and sadder he felt. The breakaway that he had wanted so badly and the independence he had hurried to attain now settled in the pit of his stomach.

From Monday night to Saturday morning, he shared the ride with a cross-section of his countrymen and countrywomen. They crossed the Mississippi River together. They saw the Southwestern ochre plateaus and tawny plains together. There were people of all ages traveling—some alone and some together. There were young families with babies before disposable diapers. Gently swaying to the rhythm of the road, they were all headed west.

Arriving in Phoenix around noon on Saturday, Fig found a hotel room and a hot shower. When Sunday morning arrived, he called the Base from the Phoenix bus depot on his way to Chandler, Arizona. There, a Base vehicle arrived to take him the short distance from Chandler to Williams AFB. The temperature was near 105 degrees. There were few trees. The tan mountain range known as the Bare White Tank Mountains replaced the southern pines and Appalachian foothills. Nashville's Cumberland River was supplanted by Phoenix's Salt River.

He was homesick and scared about his flight future. The driver of the Base vehicle did nothing for his sagging confidence.

"Are you headed to fight school?" he asked.

"Yes, Sir," was Fig's polite reply.

"Well, I pick 'em up one week and take 'em back a few months later" (referring to those individuals who hadn't made the cut).

Fig was worried. Would he washout too?

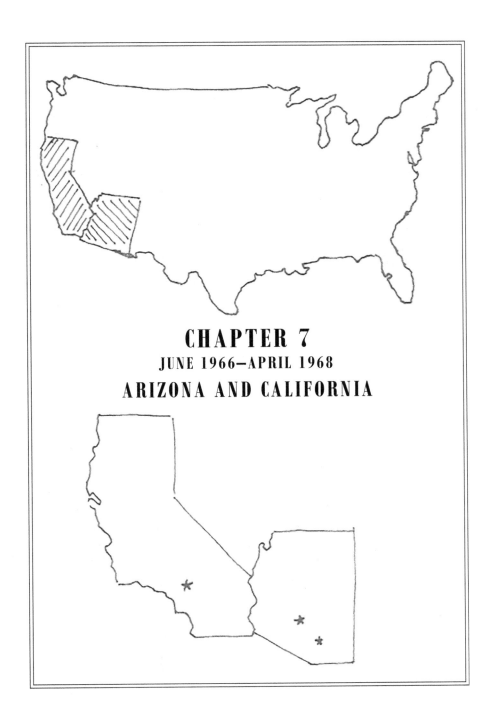

CHAPTER 7
JUNE 1966–APRIL 1968
ARIZONA AND CALIFORNIA

South Carolina's European-immigrant history began with the English colony of "Carolina" in 1665. Over two hundred years later, in 1868, Phoenix, Arizona began as a small colony called "Swillings Mill." Just as some aboriginal nations of the American Southeast had vanished before the English arrived, Arizona's ancient Pueblo Grande nation was now called "Ho Ho Kam: The People Who Have Gone."[17] South Carolina and Arizona had different histories and different centuries of their founding, yet in the twentieth century, they both became parts of Lloyd Newton's life.

Moving to the place of "The People Who Have Gone" made Newton feel that "A Way of Life Gone" would be a fitting name for his present situation. Memories of home were in sharp contrast to his new locale. He would adjust to the desert. After all, he was already used to the heat and he certainly didn't miss the Carolina humidity. But how would he adjust to the job?

Pilot training began in this Valley of the Sun. He was wearing the uniform. Now he would fight to wear the wings. The folks at Williams AFB wasted no time as academics and flight training began in earnest. The Air Force's training curriculum was very compressed and fast-paced. Each of its academic classes, such as aerodynamics, was completed in ten to twelve days, not weeks like college courses.

Fig looked at the planes on the flight line and thought back to his TSU ROTC flight lessons. He had brought his logbooks to Arizona. He was proud of the training he had already received. In the spring of 1962, freshman Newton had had his very first airplane ride. TSU owned a classic J3 Piper Cub, a consummate training aircraft in which he would take his initial flight lesson. His college flight lessons were mostly in Cessna 172s and 175s, high-wing planes.

His primary flight instructor at the university had been Cecil Ryan, a former civilian flight instructor with the Tuskegee Airmen during World War II. Ryan taught his student pilots more than just the controls. During one lesson, Fig was in the Cessna 172's left seat, the "pilot-in-command" position. Ryan noticed Fig had not fastened his seat belt. The instructor calmly took over the controls. He pulled the nose up steeply, then he jammed the nose down. Fig's head slammed into the ceiling, and then his body slammed back down into the seat. Only then did Ryan sternly order: "Put that seat belt on *now*!" Fig packed that lesson of detail and discipline along with him to Williams. He remembered it each time he climbed into the T-41, the military version of a Cessna 172, and all other airplanes he flew thereafter!

Being in the T-41 cockpit was much more intense than his college flight experiences. Unfortunately, many of the previous black student pilots from TSU and other colleges had not accumulated a very good record in this tough training environment. Perhaps expectations based on that record made things even tougher for the next group of candidates, like Fig. The fifty-three-week-long battle for those coveted wings began.

John Allen, a Tuskegee College graduate, was Fig's roommate. Being the only two black students in the flight class, they did their best to encourage each other. The academics were tough for them both. Newton's troubles became more serious in the second quarter as the class moved into T-37s. With difficult classes and his inability to develop a good rapport with his flight instructor, Fig was getting pretty scared. If he washed out in either flight training or the classroom, it was over in both. Then he would become just more fodder for that base-vehicle driver and his comments.

Failing three academic classes with any grade below 75% during the entire fifty-three-week course of study was all it took. After Fig's first failing grade, the training officer called him into the office and reviewed his academic records.

"Any questions?" the officer asked.

"No, Sir."

His superior quietly signed the forms and said, "Okay. You're dismissed."

A brief ten days later, after the second failure in only three months, Fig was back at the desk again, this time for a long discussion. All he could think about was that he had already failed twice and he still had many months to go.

The training officer reviewed the records again, this time in more detail. He paused and then asked, "Weren't you in here just a couple of weeks ago?"

"Yes, Sir," Fig replied.

"So are you studying?" asked the officer.

"Yes, Sir," Fig replied with a feeling of anger. (*Of course* he was studying!)

"*When* are you studying, Newton?" the officer continued.

Fig answered quickly, "Sir, 7:00 p.m. to approximately 2:00 a.m.," thinking that his schedule was at least disciplined even if wasn't producing success.

"When do you sleep?" was the next question.

"From 2:00 a.m. to about 5:00 a.m." was Fig's reply.

Shocked by his response, the instructor replied, "Good reason you're failing. You're not getting enough sleep. I want you to study from 7:00 p.m. to 11:00 p.m. Then no matter how much or how little you have finished, go to bed and get a good night's rest."

The officer knew that the cockpit of a high-performance aircraft and the flight-training classroom required a pilot to have the proper amount of rest to handle the pressure. With these orders and words of advice, Fig was dismissed.

Newton still remembers those two conversations with the training officer. The man offered advice and encouragement, but Fig alone had to make the grade. The training officer knew, more than Lloyd, that the demands of future cockpits would be the pilot's alone to handle. Fig now proudly declares that he never again failed a course in the United States Air Force! Key lesson: sometimes doing the very best you can means learning a new way to do it. This lesson, Newton recalls, saved his whole Air Force career!

He knew why he had been doing it, why he had been keeping those late-night hours. He was working hard so that he wouldn't let down himself, his family, TSU, and future black student pilots. He really wanted this! "I will not become another failed black student statistic," Newton still remembers promising himself.

Fig's Jasper County years had centered on family, friends, and neighborhood—his day-to-day life was lived in the black (then segregated) community. Fig's college years had centered on professors and young students striving to succeed—his life there was lived on a campus of black students. Although his summers in Boston included more integrated experiences, most of his time was still in the black community. Back in Ridgeland, there had been no white friends in Sunday School, no white children on the school bus, and very few on the Tennessee State campus. When he recalled all those earlier times throughout his life, the familiar faces had been tinted all the shades of dark, as if painted from an African savanna palette. The pigments on this new flight training canvas, though, were rapidly changing.

From 1942 until 1966, Fig had been a proven success in almost everything he had tried. (Remember, though, those crooked cornfield rows that needed re-plowing?) This success was part of his confidence, his attitude, and his drive. All of this was shaken during those first Air Force training weeks. His identity, his core sense of self, was being challenged. His successes had always been in that all-black, segregated world. That was the only world in which he had been *allowed* to succeed. When he and his roommate walked through that Air Force classroom door, they saw a new picture. For the first time, they were the lone black men in the room. It was a new world experience. Honestly, it was a new experience for most people in those early years of desegregation. For Allen and Newton, however, it was all-pervasive.

The other students were in the same culture in which they had grown up. They were a bunch of guys who already felt they were good enough to have made it this far. They were competing with each other, something else they were used to doing. Yet they didn't have to think about the advantage of the familiar *white* atmosphere in which they worked. If one of them was having a tough time, he may have only questioned his ability. However, for Fig, he questioned his ability because of his ethnicity. Fig was struggling to maintain his belief in his identity. Every time he walked into the classroom or the flight room, he would think, *We are the only two blacks in here.*

In those early days, Fig developed a constant subconscious questioning. He couldn't calm the fearful thought, *Is my brain smart enough?* This psychology stayed with Fig for months. A few flight instructors lacked confidence in the minority students. Was that attitude shaped from past minority performance or had the past minority performance been predicated by the prevailing racial attitudes of the instructors and in the country?

The mind is, thankfully, a flexible survival tool. Newton gradually adjusted. Times were what they were. It was what it was. By not quitting and by fighting to do his best, however, he corralled his internal conflicts to successfully meet the external demands. Finally he began to feel at ease. A couple of days would pass where his focus was only on class. Then a week would go by. Then a month passed. With his renewed sense of self-worth, he was better able to concentrate on what he was there to learn.

It took six to nine months of being in a white-majority environment to overcome the constant awareness of the classroom's population. He no longer saw it as a negative thing, just a new thing. At the beginning, it was in the forefront of his life, socially, emotionally, and professionally. He was now beginning to concentrate solely on the curriculum. His life-long comfort zone was being stripped away at Williams AFB. Now a new zone was replacing it. America was slowly working toward the same goal. It would just take longer.

His classmates, members of that new generation, were all adjusting to this new way of military life. They could see that this kid with the funny name had real talent. Fig was catching on at Williams AFB. He knew it, and his friends saw it. More importantly, everyone knew too that they would all end up on the same team. Their survival would depend upon each other.

One Sunday evening, an official reception was held at the Base Officers' Club to honor the student pilots. They were introduced to the base leadership and the flight instructors along with their spouses. Fig inched through the receiving line with his classmates and then got something to eat.

When he felt it was time to leave, he commented to several of his mates, "I'm gonna slip out now."

One of his classmates, flashing a big smile, said, "Newton, a lot of us in this room can just slip out of here. You're *not* one of them!" As they all laughed, they understood that the give-and-take of good humor and friendship will span many a bridge of conflict and misunderstanding.

December arrived. The first half of training was *over*! Was Fig glad to get away from Arizona and the Air Force for a while? Was he anxious to see his home and family again? Absolutely! A Christmas leave back home was just what he needed. He practiced breathing again. Celebrations included a Christmas Eve birthday with his family and Christmas presents the next day. John Newton had brought the LeMans home from Springfield, North Carolina. Sliding *carefully* back behind the wheel of his "baby" made every day even better.

Another important event happened during that holiday season. Fig's Carolina sweetheart, Miss Ruby Gadson, became Mrs. Lloyd Newton on Christmas Eve! When his leave was up, the new couple steered the beloved Pontiac westward on their cross-country honeymoon back to Arizona. They settled in an off-base apartment, then Fig began the second half of pilot training in a new aircraft.

The class now moved up to the T-38, a high-performance, Mach-one jet. A new corps of flight instructors with different attitudes welcomed them. Theirs was a more serious goal. Their students were more experienced pilots. They had passed through that first half-year of fire and survived.

The students heard: "You're adults, and now you know flying the T-38." It was time to get down to the real business of the Air Force. The war in Southeast Asia continued. More pilots, more quickly was the goal.

At that time, pilots were being trained for the back seats of F-4 Phantom jets. This was a new aircraft for the Air Force with a new approach to its use. Previously a Navy-only jet, it had been used for aircraft carrier operations. Radar personnel as weapons system officers flew in the rear seats. Now a modified version would be used by the

Air Force for air-to-air and air-to-ground operations. It was decided that having two pilots aboard would make for safer missions. Pilots formerly flying bombers, other fighters, airlifts, and many other aircraft were now filling a huge number of empty F-4 cockpits. As the conflict between North and South Vietnam continued, US military presence was increasing. Top pilots were being trained to support the US and Allied soldiers on the ground.

Simultaneously, the Civil Rights movement was making progress. The United States Air Force was determined to place qualified personnel of all races and creeds in available positions and to open the flight lines to all men with the famously named "right stuff." Did the changes come quickly? Was it a smooth transition? Like the rest of the country, the military's civil rights progress was at times shaky and slow. However, change—good change—was coming. Fig realized these new programs would only be the beginning. *(Author's note: female pilots would follow in the footsteps of and resume the service pioneered by their WWII Women Airforce Service Pilots [WASP] Sisters at a later time.)*

The year spent at Williams revealed that Fig Newton could fly—fly very well, as a matter of fact. He received his Air Force wings in June 1967 along with an aircraft assignment in an F-4 Phantom back seat. The nametag on his flight suit read "2nd Lt. Lloyd Newton." Then the military brass made further investments in Fig Newton. He was assigned first to Davis Martin AFB in Tucson, Arizona and then on to George AFB in Victorville, California, about a hundred miles northeast of Los Angeles. There in the California desert, though, they may as well have been a thousand miles away from the Hollywood glitz and glamour. George AFB was all business. Fig never did get to any of those big-time Hollywood movie studios just down the road.

Almost all of the Victorville flight instructors had served one or two tours in Vietnam. For six months, Fig's primary front-seat pilot was Major Robert (Bob) Lindeke. Bob was just coming out of the University of Wyoming where he had been studying for his master's degree. He had not flown in several years and had never flown fighters. Being a former B-47 bomber pilot, however, meant he was used to working with a crew in the aircraft. The two of them flew almost all their missions together during that time. Fig learned a lot about flying, a lot about combat, and a lot about surviving.

Halfway through his five months at George AFB, he became First Lieutenant Newton. When he left California, he thoroughly knew the business of the F-4D fighter. February 1968—the months of training were ending. On leave, he drove Ruby back to South Carolina and family. Next, he reported to Fairchild AFB, Spokane, Washington, for two weeks of basic survival training in the frigid hills of the Northwest.

The intensity of the national racial conflict was not as strong among this close-knit group of young men who were about to put their lives on the line for their country. They knew, however, that things were still very different "off base." A great friend in pilot training, Sam Spayd, had come up to Fig at their graduation. "I really wish it were possible for you to come visit me at home in Mississippi." They both understood the bittersweetness in that statement. Time would change that, they prayed.

With the last of the training behind him, Fig was invited to join six friends from survival school and pilot training to stay in San Francisco for a few days before they left for Vietnam. On Tuesday, April 2, 1968, he was about to deploy, so it was time for one last party in downtown San Francisco.

Two days later, Fig was scheduled to fly out around midnight from Travis AFB, California. In the middle of that Thursday afternoon, he was still in downtown San Francisco. A group of friends came to find him. Their mood was unusually solemn. They started apologizing as they gathered around him. He didn't know what was going on, but he knew something was definitely wrong.

It was April 4, 1968. They had come to tell him that American Civil Rights leader, Dr. Martin Luther King Jr., had been assassinated at the Lorraine Motel in Memphis, Tennessee. Throughout this nation's history—from its fight for independence in the 1700s, through the bitter Civil War in the 1800s, and on to the struggle for civil rights in the 1900s—each century's changes have been accompanied by confusion, conflict, divergent perspectives, heated dialogue, and sadly, often unwanted violence. Why does it so often have to go that far?

Those friends, standing there around him, asked quietly, "What will you do, Newton, if the government and the military turn against your people?" He thought of the oath he had sworn to "support and defend the Constitution of the United States against all enemies, foreign and domestic."[18] He also thought about who the enemy in this situation may be. Lloyd had been raised a worker, a doer, a person of action. What choices could, should, or would he make for his future and the future of those around him? It was a very confusing time for this young black man from South Carolina.

Later that same night, very somberly, he climbed aboard the chartered commercial aircraft for Clark Air Base, Philippines on his way to Southeast Asia. He wondered to himself whether the war was in Vietnam or here in America. He did know, however, that he had made his commitment and had his orders. He felt that he must honor that commitment because that was the Newton way.

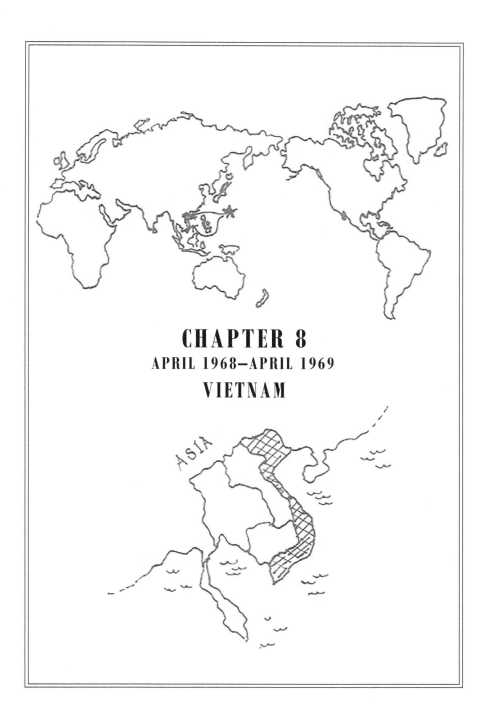

CHAPTER 8
APRIL 1968–APRIL 1969
VIETNAM

In the days leading up to his deployment, 1ˢᵗ Lieutenant Newton had thought about how to best use the long hours on the flight crossing the Pacific. He made a mental checklist: *rest*, review his training, *rest*, relax, stay focused. There were so many things to think about. He was headed into a war zone, and there were plenty of reasons to believe he might not make it back. Every day, the television news reported the number of Americans killed in the war. Fig paid close attention to the number of lost planes. He planned to enjoy the calm and quiet of the flight. When he walked off the plane onto a new continent, he must be ready for the next set of pressures.

The events at Memphis' Lorraine Motel and the loss of Dr. King changed those on-board plans. By the time the plane touched down at Clark Air Base in the Philippines, the shock of the assassination had turned to a deep, numb pain in Lloyd's heart. He was on his way to South Vietnam, though, so that had to be his priority and focus for now.

Newly arrived fliers stayed at Clark about a week. They were kept busy while their internal clocks were adjusting to the new time. Most important on the agenda that week was a jungle survival course. The physical environment of the Philippines was closer to that of South Vietnam than was any place in the United States. Both an American military instructor and an indigenous Negrito Tribe[19] instructor led the course. The Negritos were masters of how to survive off the land. They taught many lessons on escape, evasion, and survival using whatever resources were available. Knowing what to expect from nature made the pilots better prepared to concentrate on what was coming from the enemy.

If one finds South Carolina on a globe, carefully moves a finger straight up, over the North Pole, and then down again it will come to Vietnam. That's fairly close to being on the opposite side of the world from Ridgeland. These two geographic areas have both historically supported large-scale rice production. The majority of Carolina's production was discontinued toward the end of the nineteenth century. Vietnam continues its rice production today. The area's lower latitude makes Southeast Asia more tropical than the South Carolina low-country flat woods and marshes. Their similar climates, however, share humidity-laden heat that encourages insects to rise up in search of tender skin to torture. Those modern rice fields, called rice paddies, played a large role in military strategies throughout the Vietnam conflict, almost always to the detriment of the United States and its Allies and the benefit of the enemy.

Tan Son Nhut was the primary Allied military base and home to the American Embassy in Saigon. At that time, it was the second busiest airport in the world, just after Chicago's O'Hare. US Army, Navy, Marine, Air Force, and South Vietnamese aircraft shared the runways around the clock. During the previous night, just hours before Fig's plane had arrived, Viet Cong-launched rockets had hit the airport terminal. An American pilot who was on his way home after flying a hundred combat missions over the North was killed. The runways and buildings wore the holes and scars of the rocket attacks. *This is the real war,* Fig thought. He saw it everywhere he looked. That April afternoon, Fig and his teammates didn't stay long at Tan Son Nhut. They flew on to Da Nang Air Base on a C-130 cargo aircraft.

It was late on a Sunday evening. He grabbed his duffle bag and marched off in his flight suit to assigned quarters, located close to a main road. Thundering tanks roared by at all hours, spewing up dust that settled into and over everything. This was where he would "rest" between missions.

During his first week at Da Nang, four F-4 Phantoms were shot down in five days. Only one two-pilot crew was rescued. Those in the other three planes, six men, were either dead or MIA (Missing In Action). There rarely seemed to be a time when only *one* aircraft would be lost in the same night or two nights in a row. Things always seemed to happen in "threes," and it always seemed to be someone he knew. Fig thought to himself, *With these odds, it doesn't look good for me returning home.*

After his first week of in-country orientation, Fig checked the flying schedule and found that he was scheduled for his first mission. It would be over North Vietnam. His immediate thought was, why did his first mission have to be up north? Why not down over South Vietnam where the enemy fire would be less intense and he could get a feel for combat? It was not to be. The next day, he was teamed with Major Rex Hammock, an experienced fighter pilot and combat veteran. The Major was flying his ninety-fourth mission over the North. He needed only six more to complete his tour and head home. Then there was rookie Newton. This was a two-ship sortie with a tasking order to strike a military storage facility near the Quang Khe River in North Vietnam.

When Hammock and Newton took the first dive bombing run at the target, Fig was concentrating so completely on the altitude and attitude of the F-4 aircraft that he didn't even recognize the flak smoke from the enemy gunfire going off all around them. During the dive for the bomb pass, Fig would call off the aircraft altitude and call "pickle" when it was time to release the bombs. "12,000, 11, 10, 9,000, pickle, pickle," called Fig.

Rex would depress the pickle button, releasing all six 750-pound bombs, then pull the aircraft out of the dive and away from the target. After the bomb run, Hammock would "jink" the aircraft (make a quick evasive turn) to confuse the North Vietnamese gunner who may be tracking them. Then he asked Fig, "Do you see that flak?"

Fig looked around outside and asked, "Where?"

Rex pointed out the little puffs of smoke in the sky all around their aircraft. Fig had never seen flak (the explosion of gunfire) before and hadn't known what to look for.

Fig flew a total of 269 missions, most often with Major Bob Lindeke, his aircraft commander from their training days back at George AFB. They made a very effective team. They flew sorties over North Vietnam together, and thankfully, they flew home together, too. They have remained close friends over the years, even after Lindeke retired from the Air Force.

Their missions included support of ground troops—escorting B-52s and C-123s, stopping ground supply shipments, and air-to-air combat. The canals and wetlands of the countryside were dotted with dams to control the water in the rice paddies. The Viet Cong (North Vietnam soldiers) placed anti-aircraft guns atop many of these embankments for better aim at the American aircraft overhead because the US ROE (Rules of Engagement) prohibited bombing these embankments. This resulted in the loss of several aircraft and crews. The intensity of war never let up. Many flights were flown under cover of darkness, but that seldom provided much in the way of safety.

By the time Fig arrived in April 1968, President Lyndon B. Johnson had limited the scope of US military bombing. By Thanksgiving of '68, the President had banned all bombing over the North except for some special missions. This decision meant that Fig would fly relatively few missions across the North Vietnam border. That changed his plan to reach his goal of 100 enemy-territory missions over North Vietnam by Christmas and head home early.

Captain Steve Ritchie, who would later become one of five Air Force "Aces" of the Vietnam conflict, was in his first Vietnam tour.[20] He and Fig took off one night in bad weather. The radar in their wingman's aircraft went out, and their radio was having difficulty as well, so the two planes aborted (called off) the mission and headed back to Da Nang. As Steve and Fig positioned for their final approach, the control tower reported that the airport was under a bombing attack by enemy ground rockets set up just outside the airfield. Ritchie landed, pulled the F-4 onto a taxiway, and popped the canopies. Deplaning, both pilots ran to an adjacent ditch for cover. Seconds later, they recalled that although the rockets were not very accurate, most of them usually landed between the runways. Both men started running for their lives across the runway to hopeful safety. A major part of the memory of that night for Newton was that run. Steve Ritchie had been a halfback at the US Air Force Academy. They were both flat-out sprinting, but Fig definitely lagged behind his speedy teammate!

Everybody loved getting news from home. Fig had only been away a few months when, in July, the Red Cross tried unsuccessfully to deliver an emergency message. When their attempts failed, the

Air Force stepped in. Using two-way MARS radio, the message got through. On July 21, 1968, Lloyd W. Newton *Junior* was born in the Beaufort Naval Hospital in Beaufort, South Carolina. Fig and Ruby had a son! Fig just *had* to make it back home! Dr. King's dream for America's children now included his own.

When he climbed out of a Phantom after a mission, Fig's body was hot, tired, and aching. His mind was exhausted. He remembered feeling like that as a boy. Back then, he'd have to fight the temptation to give up and walk away from all that hard work, but the fear of disappointing his parents kept him going. Those early lessons of commitment had slowly settled deep within him. Now when the jungle-sticky heat and the hot-metal smells crowded his brain, he would draw out those memories for reinforcement.

One does not experience war without fear. "There were missions I was really scared," Fig would comment later. As a pilot, he was deeply touched by the dangerous conditions under which the ground troops served. He would have made every one of his missions a troops-in-contact support effort if he could have chosen. "I sure was glad I was up in the air and not down there with those ground troops," he often remembered. He was always glad to be flying those types of missions.

(Years later, Newton would make this comment in a speech for the Armed Forces Staff College: "One day after reading the rules of engagement update for my next mission, I thought, *It's a war! It's hard for rules and paper to argue with enemy defenses and the hair standing up on the back of your neck.)*

Flying at night was always tough. When refueling in bad weather, the night got even darker. The pilots were always relieved when they could disconnect the refueling probe and continue on. Often a mission would send them over Laos. They would provide cover for helicopters as they flew in to rescue troops. On one of those flights, twelve to twenty birds were circling the area, making flying more dangerous but beautiful. Nature's miracles coexisted with war's destruction. Later in his tour, he sometimes flew with new "front-seaters" on their theater indoctrination missions. On those days, his combat experience made him feel war-zone old.

The troops were well aware of what was going on back in the States. The pilots, however, had developed an unspoken pact. They knew what their priority had to be. In their daily conversations, they deliberately steered away from topics of civil rights and anti-war conflicts on the home front. They could do nothing about it half a world away. They had to stay focused on the cohesiveness of the team.

When he had some spare time alone, Fig would think to himself, *Who and what am I?* His conclusions would have been very different had he not served abroad. The conflicts that raged in America were very real. However, a *"big"* (Newton's own emphasis) turning point in his world view came from a Vietnamese family living just outside the perimeter of the base. A man, woman, and one child lived right at the edge of the road in a five-foot-by-ten-foot dwelling of old boards covered by a plastic tarp. They cooked all their meals outside with whatever fuel they could find. At night, they would close the plastic-tarp door. Each day the man would ride his scooter to his security job. Fig watched this family for the whole year. He carries that sober mental picture to this day. That experience made it very clear to Fig that he was fortunate to be an American.

Time for growing up is a luxury not afforded by war. The young warrior-man knew one thing for certain: America wasn't perfect, and it definitely had its problems. He could, though, be part of the solution. He would "return home and enjoy all the freedoms and opportunities America *should* offer to all its citizens." When thinking of home, as bad as it was in those turbulent '60s, he had seen worse. He knew his nation was still the best. He hadn't always felt like that, but he now had day-to-day real-life comparisons to address the cultural conflicts he had to live through.

"Who am I? I'm an American. I will go back and work to make the best better. I will serve the Air Force and the nation and help to make them even better," the war-weary pilot decided.

Everybody was homesick. What did Fig miss most? At the top of his list were his own brand-new family, his extended family, friends from all over, real milk, real eggs, the clean comforts of home, squadron mates back in the United States and *quiet*!

Some years in life pass slowly and others quickly. That Vietnam year could not pass any too soon for Lloyd's family and the families of all service men and women. They stayed behind, lifting up their prayers for safe returns. The troops longed for the trip home too. The plane flying them out of Da Nang was given its own name by the troops—"Freedom Bird." Finally it was Newton's turn to board. He had flown 269 combat missions out of Da Nang, 79 of them over North Vietnam.

April to April. Was it only a year or was it a lifetime? For many, it tragically became both as Fig lost several of his friends in Vietnam—some captured, some killed. He was finally headed back to the United States of America. The flight took the airmen through Alaska, over Anchorage, down the North American coast to Norton AFB, San Bernardino, California. Home Sweet Home! When they landed around 9:00 a.m., California time, almost every person on that plane ran down the ramp, knelt down, and kissed the ground. They were so thankful to be back on American soil.

He couldn't wait for his commercial flight from Los Angeles to Savannah. There they all were! His family stood waiting to see him with Ruby and baby Lloyd Jr. in the front. All of a sudden, from around the back of the group, John Newton rushed forward, past Ruby and the baby, past Annie, past everyone. He ran up to Lloyd and gave him a big bear hug. His son was home! His boy was safely home! Fig couldn't believe this expression of love from a reserved man who was never one for displays of that kind of affection. Annie, of course, hustled John back out of the way so that Fig could welcome his wife and finally meet that new son! Little Lloyd Jr., born when his daddy was half-a-world away, cried when the tall stranger took him in his pilot-strong arms. But that was all right. They would have thirty days of leave to get to know each other. And Fig would *never* forget his daddy's welcome-home hug.

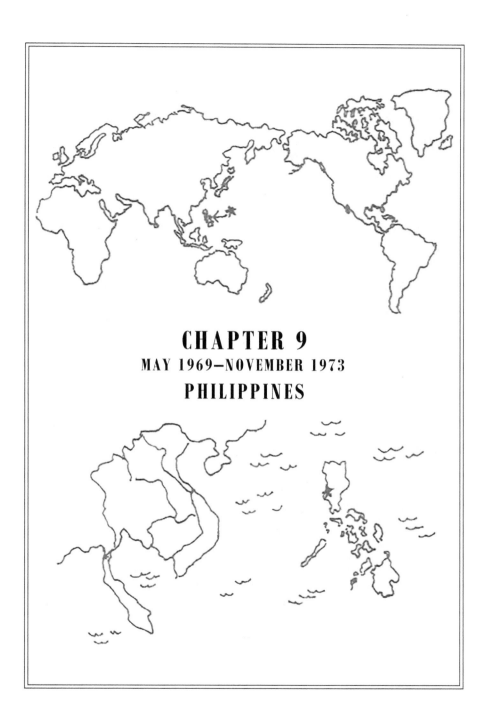

CHAPTER 9
MAY 1969–NOVEMBER 1973
PHILIPPINES

Vietnam had not been the only scene of conflict during Fig's year away. Soldiers returning from Southeast Asia were met with vocal anti-war protests. Widespread demonstrations for racial equality filled the streets. Newton, like other new veterans, had served his country, lived up to his commitment, and put his life on the line. Once back home, however, he was often not afforded the most common forms of respect and courtesy from his fellow citizens. Black service members were questioned about fighting for a country that did not offer them the same freedoms as others. Fig could see that the Air Force gave him the best opportunity to influence others to help improve racial equality throughout the ranks.

During his thirty-day leave, Fig decided to visit his sister, Dottie, and the rest of his family in Boston. From there, he went to New York City to visit his cousin, Carl Smith and other relatives. Carl and Fig were exactly one year and one day apart in age. (Fig was born December 24, 1942; Carl was born December 25, 1943.) They were as close as brothers, growing up together, even starting school at the same time. After Carl, a brilliant man, completed his junior college degree, he joined Harry and Fig at Tennessee State.

One night during the New York visit, a siren went off outside the house. Fig hit the floor—and fast! His first Vietnam War flashback had surprised and upset them all. For Fig, it was a natural warzone survival reaction during an attack.

The month of leave passed quickly. In May, Fig, Ruby, and Lloyd Jr. started west again. This time, the LeMans carried them back to George Air Force Base, California.

The business there had not changed. For the next five months, Newton received upgraded front-seat qualification training for the F-4D. He was in the air night and day, five to six days a week. "You are commander of this aircraft to test its capabilities." And test it he did. He was rapidly adding flight hours to his logbook, along with experience and knowledge. Some days he would look back and smile. Before the Air Force and before the planes, when he was a student or a part-time worker, he never wanted Mondays to come. That marked the beginning of another workweek. Now he couldn't wait to get to work. He loved flying so much he would volunteer to do weekend maintenance test flights. "When you're doing something you really love, you'll do it anytime. This was dreams coming true," he remembers.

In mid-June, he was promoted to captain. The Air Force asked for his three top choices for his next duty location. He wanted Thailand, a location, he joked, that was used for "commuting to the war" because it was just outside the Vietnam War zone. He had contributed once; he wanted to return.

During a "discussion" regarding his next assignment versus where he thought he *should* go, he was adamant. "I'm going to Thailand! Go back and tell them, Sergeant. I don't want to go to the Philippines!"

The next day, the sergeant was back. "Well, Captain, have you thought about the assignment anymore?"

"Yes," replied Fig, "and I am still going to Thailand."

"What would you say to your family, Captain, if you got shot down?" Fig was taken aback. He had never thought of it that way. The sergeant grabbed Fig's attention with his pointed remark.

"Okay, I'll go to Clark." (*And then I'll go to Thailand*, he thought to himself.) The Philippines it was. He'd be staying a little longer this time than he did after his first arrival.

The Philippines archipelago consists of 7,107 islands, only 40% of which are named. The large islands are divided into three geographical districts. To the north is Luzon. The Visayan Islands form the center, and Mindanao is to the south. Originally inhabited for thousands of years by ancient peoples of Asian descent, it has hosted many cultures. Its first European contact was in 1521 during the historic first global circumnavigation by the Spanish explorer, Ferdinand Magellan. It was named after Philip II of Spain.

Later a territory of the United States, it became a self-governing commonwealth on November 15, 1935, with a ten-year goal of tran-

sitioning to full independence. World War II came to the Pacific shortly afterward when the Japanese attacked the United States at Pearl Harbor on December 7, 1941. The ensuing war years saw battle after battle for control and occupation of these islands. Both Japan and the Allies controlled this strategic location at various times. It was a violent time for the Filipino people. At the end of the war, the United States again played a major role in the islands' path toward self-rule. On July 4, 1946, the Republic of the Philippines celebrated its full independence.[21]

Located in the tropical Pacific Ocean and on the eastern hemisphere's geologic "Ring of Fire," the nation is subject to both typhoons and earthquakes. The richness of its biodiversity makes it one of the most beautiful places in the world.

In November '69, Newton returned to Clark AB where he began the longest tour of duty in his career thus far. The air base was near Angeles City on the northern island of Luzon. When his first assignment was up, he requested an extension. In the Philippines, Fig found a philosophy of "people are people." With all the strife back in the States, it was a refreshing outlook. Filipinos were great neighbors, helpful friends, and hard workers.

His family lived off base where Ruby had a housekeeper to help with the house and the baby, a gardener to help in the yard, and friends to watch out for them while Fig was away. When stationed outside the United States, the squadron becomes the service personnel's extended family. Many traveled together to enjoy the Philippine culture.

Within a year, the Newton family welcomed a new little one. Cheryl was born on July 31, 1970. Although Lloyd Jr. was born when Fig was at Da Nang, this time Daddy was right there in the Clark AB hospital room. Ruby handled the household and the children. She wanted to support Fig in any way she could. She would be sure his uniforms and civilian clothes were in perfect order so that her husband would look the part of the disciplined pilot and leader that he was. She was one of those committed "non-uniform service personnel," otherwise known as a military wife, who stepped up to any role that helped her family. Fig was flying. His family was together. They now had a boy and a girl. "Life was great!" Fig recalls. It was a memorable four years.

Having worked so hard when he was growing up, Fig was especially respectful of the Filipino people's resourcefulness. They used whatever they had to create beauty. He remembers one man's intricately carved design on a long beam, all done by hand with only a small chisel and hammer. What really amazed Fig was that the man had no blueprint or plan of any kind. Like an artist, the creation flowed from within.

From a political standpoint, Newton viewed the Ferdinand Marcos-led government of that time as one of weak leadership, not responsive to the social and economic needs of the people. The people had very few resources and little voice over the power elite. This weakness would lead to further unrest and eventual removal of Marcos from power.

Clark Air Base's mission was to provide direct defense of the host country and nearby Allied nations. Being at Clark was all about flying. All of the pilots did it. They did it because there was a war in their backyard. This created a better pilot atmosphere, one in which there was no time or place for the pilot swagger sometimes found on other bases. Flying was the job to be done. Fig appreciated this atmosphere of aviation humility.

The 523rd Fighter Squadron to which Fig was assigned had an alert commitment in support of the Taiwanese government against China. The pilots also trained to respond to any emergency in the Pacific and to rapidly deploy to Vietnam if needed. Once a month, Fig would be on alert in Tainan, Taiwan for a week. Two F-4 aircraft from the 523rd with certified crews sat "a five-minute alert." This meant that if the horn sounded, they were airborne in five minutes. This procedure was rehearsed around the clock and *often*! The Taiwan alert tour for each crew lasted from Friday to Friday.

One day while he was in Tainan, an announcement came over the facility intercom. "Newton, you've got a phone call." Wing Commander James (Jim) Tilton was on the line.

In 1971 and 1972, Clark and other Asian bases were experiencing racial tensions just like those stateside. In the recent past, conflicts and riots had occurred on several military locations, both at home and abroad. In 1972, a takeover of the dining hall in a protest at Laredo AFB, Texas, forced the Air Force into immediate action. A letter was sent out by Chief of Staff of the Air Force, General John D. Ryan, to all commands: "I desire that you, your commanders and supervisors support the USAF Equal Opportunity and Race Relations Education program with the same vigor and enthusiasm as that given the flying mission" (Letter of October 18, 1972).

"Fig, this is Jim Tilton," drawled the Texan. "I need somebody to be in command of our Equal Opportunity and Treatment (EOT) program. It's a new DOD (Department of Defense) program dealing with racial issues in the military. Washington knows we need to educate our military men and women on what we have in common as Americans."

This had never been done before. The military was good with discipline and punishment, but each case was not always handled in the same manner. The main tension was between black and white; however, other minorities were having issues as well. Reporting was not always done in a consistent manner. In one instance, statistical numbers regarding discipline had been changed to make them look better for a briefing to top brass. When discovered, the officer responsible was dismissed. The word was out. The Air Force was taking this new directive and approach to equal opportunity seriously.

The time had finally arrived for action. Lloyd "Fig" Newton was put right into the *heart* and the *heat* of it. The prototype program would be at Clark. During a visit there by Undersecretary of Defense Frank Render, he and his team met with officers, non-commissioned officers, blacks, whites, Hispanics, men, and women. They concluded there was a desperate need for people to have a venue in which to talk to and talk through these tense times.

Fig jumped in with enthusiastic trepidation. He hadn't wanted this assignment (after all, he was a *pilot!*), but it was his now. James Tilton had known this was going to be a tough project, so he had respectfully made a personal call to Fig to tell him about it. Newton noticed and remembered the commander's kind gesture. Fig had his orders, and he would carry them out fully. Working with a committed team, they organized "salt and pepper" personnel into two two-man teams. Team One had one black officer and one white non-commissioned officer (NCO). Team Two had one white officer and one black NCO. One secretary/assistant worked on the administrative details for both teams. The group wrote a curriculum to meet specific goals. Class schedules were set for all mid-level to senior-level personnel on the base. They started with the Base leadership: from staff sergeants to full colonels. Then the schedules went out.

Classes were held twice weekly. The twenty-five- to thirty-person groups consisted of selected cross-sections of the base population. The three-star commanding officer introduced each class. The Air Force message was clear: Listen up! This is important. This is serious. "We want you to be able to sit down and talk to each other about these (racial/cultural) issues and tell us what you think the problems are. Then give us your recommendations on how to resolve them." The class participants gradually developed a sense of trust with one another and began to have open and honest dialogues.

This was now the 1970s. Black airmen and non-commissioned officers in the classes were influenced not only by Dr. King's legacy but also by contemporary individuals and groups more vocal about racial issues. These included the Black Panthers, a militant-thinking group of young black activists, Malcolm X, Stokeley Carmichael, and H Rap Brown. Sitting in class beside them were white officers and non-commissioned officers with long years of service. They were steeped in one of segregation's most pervasive results: it had created people who were color-blocked when they should have been color-blind. Many in the class thought, and some said, "I do not want to be here. I don't need to be here."

Knowing they would be playing to a really tough crowd, Fig's team had to find a way to ease into the program. They decided that a popular television series at the time had just the person to help. *I Spy* starred Bill Cosby (a black actor) and Robert Culp (a white actor). This hadn't happened on a major network before. The Department of Defense asked Culp to star in a film specifically produced for the Air Force and DOD. It highlighted discrimination in America, and it never failed to break the initial tension.

Twice a week for one-and-a-half years, young Capt. Newton worked with all levels of personnel. Every six months, the Pacific EOT teams would meet to review their training methods and learn from each another's successes and mistakes. Their report was forwarded to DOD in Washington and dispersed to Air Force bases throughout the United States and the world.

Prominent Air Force attorney, Lieutenant Colonel Bernie Waxstein, taught classes pertaining to military justice, administrative discipline (Article 15) and court martials. Depending upon each situation, a commander could use Article 15 at his discretion for anything from a written record of offense added to an individual's personnel file all the way up to time in jail. Waxstein would display a base's statistics of previous Article 15s and court-martial trials received by airmen at that location. There would be two to three times more punishments for black airmen than there were for their fellow white counterparts. He would then challenge the class, "What do you think about these numbers? Do you see anything wrong with this? Do you think justice is being served here?"

"Waxstein was so much ahead of his time on this particular issue. Lawyers around the Air Force started researching the data and asking these questions initiated by him. That was one phenomenal team of people we had," Newton remembers.

Coming up with programs to maintain interest and promote open communication was always a challenge. Fig helped to organize the first African-American History celebration held at Clark AB. Later, at a Lackland AFB, Texas luncheon in 2008, he explained it this way:

"We got together, and we spread a little of our black culture all around. We had white folks singing gospel songs. We had collard greens and sweet potatoes and all kinds of things folks *claimed* they didn't know anything about."

It may seem stereotypical today, but back then it was a groundbreaking start to bridging a cultural divide. The real purpose of the gathering was accomplished. "It was the *first* time we got people to really talk to each other and to engage in a conversation about their heritage: where we were different and a whole lot more about where we were the same…it changed the landscape for military forces."

Fig knew they were making progress when a group of white airmen came to him with, "We want to do a rock concert." This was the '70s, and rock concerts were *big*, especially in the States. They teamed up with a group of black airmen to build a consensus of support. Together they asked Fig to be the leader and present the idea to the commander. "You'll have riots!" was the commander's first response. But Fig and the group prevailed.

Talk about a stressful undertaking! First, everyone was invited—military, families, and Filipino civilians alike. It had to be all-inclusive. The base's large park served as a great venue for the event. Preparations began. The young enlisted men, Airmen 1 and 2 "Stripers," did the majority of the planning and hard labor. It had been their idea, and they wanted to do their best to make it a success.

Next came the biggest risk, or leap of faith, depending upon one's perspective. The young people made a strong request: no police presence. "We'll police ourselves. There's no need for security forces present." Fig figuratively "leapt," keeping the security officers in the background, on stand-by only if he needed them. His only demand of the airmen: *no* alcohol.

The concert stage went up. Approximately 15,000 people showed up. From twelve noon until dark, Filipino rock bands rocked the stage. Talented GIs and their guitars joined in, playing everything from Howling Wolf and Janis Joplin to James Brown and Willie Nelson. The cleanup team showed up immediately afterward. By the next day, there was little evidence of the great party from the day before. There were no fights, no unruly behavior, and no arrests.

It was a concert. It was a festival. It was an unqualified success!

The EOT program didn't always go smoothly. It was often fraught with individual issues. Lt. Jerry Pope, a white officer from Richmond, Virginia was assigned to handle black/white issues of conflict. He had some pretty tough days. People could report instances of discrimination or mistreatment to the EOT. The personnel who had been reported would be investigated, followed by consequences where appropriate. Pope had the same message for everyone: "These are the rules: no racially inflammatory words are allowed, starting with the "*N*" word…this is mandated for whites and blacks."

Lieutenant General Marvin McNickle added even more emphasis. "The world is changing, and you're going to change with it or you won't be in the Air Force." He reinforced Lt. Pope's directive with "Not on *my* base!" McNickle was a true gentleman with no swagger, no yelling. His quiet expectation of immediate compliance produced results. Capt. Newton learned a tremendous amount from the General's strength of character.

Fig had a personal realization coming from this assignment: he was an asset to his Air Force and his country. He looked at the power he had been given to manage. He acknowledged the leadership people saw in him. It was a sobering revelation to be carrying such responsibility. Like Solomon, he prayed for wisdom.

The Equal Opportunity and Treatment project made great strides toward mutual understanding. The message was getting out. "If people don't feel valued, you're gonna have a problem." At Clark, everyone was realizing: "Okay. I'm gonna get a fair shake here." No longer were there two sides of the dining room at the Enlisted Club. Now black and white airmen sat and ate together. It made Fig smile.

The larger goal was for this training to stay with the veterans when they returned home. They would then, hopefully, choose to incorporate it into their families and communities. The theme, "What's the Fuss About in America," started discussions and changed attitudes.

The military's EOT program today has transitioned from solely black/white issues to other cultural, lifestyle, and gender issues. Today called "Social Actions," it is still responding to the many problems needing to be solved in the 21st century military. Current issues must be dealt with head-on in the struggle for social justice.

Meanwhile, *Pilot* Newton was as busy as ever. He had missed flying with his squadron on the Taiwan alert that week when he took the wing commander's fateful call. Soon after that, he transitioned to Clark's T-33 squadron. During this same time frame, his old F-4 squadron was deployed to Thailand, without Capt. Newton. His "secret plan" to go from Clark to Thailand and back to the war wasn't going to happen after all.

The T-33's job was to serve as a target for air defense training. In this aircraft, he garnered more experience in formation flying and fly-bys. Between the F-4 Phantom and T-33 assignments in the Philippines, Fig was building those flight hours. This was all part of his plan.

He kept telling everyone, "I'm going to apply to the Thunderbirds." And then, after hearing it so much, everyone started answering, "Newton, you can't stop talking about the Thunderbirds." The application required a thousand flight hours. Fig was still a bit short of that, so he was in the air as often as possible.

One day, he got a call from Flight Commander Capt. Jim Fowler. "A friend of mine, Major Bill Elander, is here. I want you to meet this guy." Elander was passing through the Philippines on his way to Thailand for the war. Come to find out, Elander was a former T-bird pilot. Fowler had told Elander of Fig's obsession, so Bill asked, "When are you going to send in that application?"

"Next year when I have my thousand hours."

"No. I recommend you send it in this year," Elander suggested. "Make the changes (update your application) and send it in now. Come by my room tomorrow with your application." Bill helped Fig hone the resume to the major's satisfaction, making sure it had the right tone and structure. Then off it went. Well, Fig had done it!

Shortly thereafter, in the fall of 1972, Fig received an early-morning phone call from the Thunderbirds. "Congratulations. You made the semifinals, and we want you to travel with the team so that we can meet and interview you."

Fig was thrilled! He jumped at the opportunity. He was greatly disappointed, however, when he learned that the semi-finals were as far as he had made it. He applied the next year and made it all the way to the finals. Again, he didn't make the final cut. Not giving up got harder each time he was passed over, but Fig still planned to try again and again until he made the team or ran out of eligibility.

As his Pacific Rim tour was winding down, Fig thought back to that 1968 flight to Clark on the day of Dr. King's assassination. Remembering his inner conflict, he knew he was now contributing to both the Air Force and his country. He and other Americans, serving around the world, were becoming closer, more understanding compatriots. They were preparing to lead the nation in new, right directions. However, Fig and those with whom he served knew there was still real work to be done on this journey for equal rights. Human nature would make it difficult to complete such a lofty goal, but the hope was that there would be enlightened progress as the nation marched toward equality.

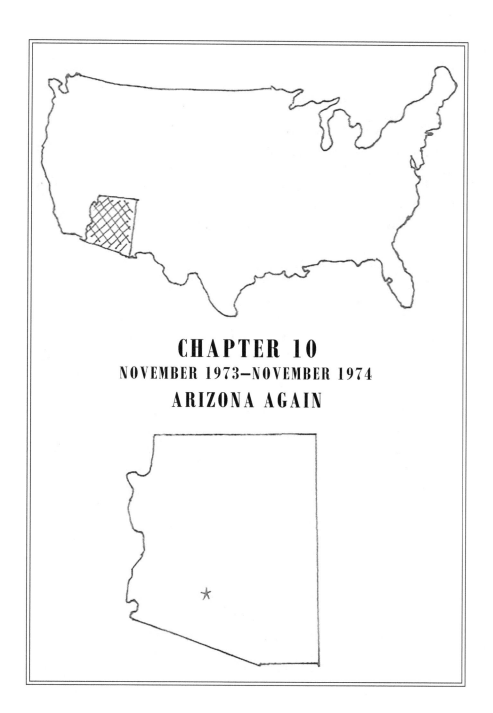

CHAPTER 10
NOVEMBER 1973–NOVEMBER 1974
ARIZONA AGAIN

After living in the South Pacific Rim for nearly five years, it was time to return to the western hemisphere. The Air Force was going to put Newton's one thousand-plus hours of flight experience to good use. He gazed out the plane's window as it lifted off the Clark Air Base runway that November 1973. It was a runway he knew well. It had felt the wheels of his F-4D and T-33 on numerous sorties. The mountainous, tropical habitat below was still as beautiful as when he first arrived.

Crossing the Pacific is never a quick flight, but on this trip, the father of two shared in his toddlers' flying excitement. He also managed to get a little rest as he thought about his sixth assignment—F-4 Phantom flight instructor pilot at Luke Air Force Base, Arizona. Returning to the state where he had received his first Air Force pilot training straight out of Tennessee State, now he would be the instructor. The planes would be just a bit more sophisticated at Luke than those early T-37 and T-38 trainers. While reluctant to leave their Filipino friends, he and his family were glad to be heading back to the US mainland.

At 30,000 feet, Fig couldn't shake the dream from his Tiger-years—the one born in the 1964 Nashville skies. How he still wanted it—that beauty of precision flight he had seen on that first Thunderbird Day! He was disappointed when others tried to discourage him. There had never been a black pilot on the Thunderbird Team. He had heard that a lot! Now with two applications and two rejections, the sharp edge of disappointment was sliding into his confidence. Fig still believed, though, that lots of "never beens" were now becoming "why nots" in his changing America. After all, he had made it to the semis once and the finals once. Should he apply this season and chance getting cut again?

Once at Luke, he had no time to worry about it. Right from the start, he loved what he was doing. Being an Instructor Pilot (IP) in the F-4 Phantom would end up being one of the best Air Force jobs he ever had. Fighter pilots want to *fly*! Capt. Newton was doing plenty of that.

The now family of four settled into their new home. Three-year-old Cheryl loved chasing her five-year-old big brother. He was getting ready for kindergarten and about to start his own generation of Newton KNOW. It was a good time to be together and to be home again. Fig and Ruby definitely missed the domestic help they had enjoyed in the Philippines, but living in Arizona, the "Valley of the Sun," was a nice alternative. It became even nicer the following June. Baby sister Lori joined the family. Just as Dorothy had been John and Annie's only girl, it looked like Lloyd Jr. would be an only brother outrunning his two little sisters.

T-Bird application time rolled around. Hesitantly, Fig looked at the calendar. Then he opened the file and reviewed his old resumes. "Do I really want to do this?" He considered sitting out a year and trying again later.

"Where's your application, Newton?" It was Steve Mish on the phone. A former competitor for a previous position (which Mish had won), he and Fig had nonetheless become friends. This time he was calling with encouragement. "Get that application in," he reiterated at the end of their conversation.

Lloyd looked back on all those boyhood times he had wanted to quit, but he hadn't. What if he didn't make it *again*? But what if he didn't even try? What would he do after another rejection? Well, he did know the answer to that question. He would concentrate on being the very best USAF F-4 flight instructor that he possibly could.

The envelope was in the mail.

This time, Fig made it to the Thunderbird Team semi-finals. He knew that drill—been there. Then he made it to the final round. Done that before, too. Next, he was at Nellis AFB, Nevada, flying in a practice flight with the team. Finally, the time came for the personal interview. "We'll call you and let you know the results," Fig heard as he walked out the door. He wasn't going to hold his breath. He headed back to Arizona.

Let's get back to work, he told himself. Back at Luke, 1974 was speeding by as quickly as the Phantoms flew. On a crisp November day in the middle of the afternoon Fig and Charles DeBellevue, a Vietnam F-4 backseat Ace, were doing a training flight on the gunnery range. Chuck DeBellevue was in the process of upgrading to the F-4 front seat. Over the radio came: "Newton, the Thunderbirds called and want you to call back." Up front, Chuck had heard the transmission too. Fig acknowledged the call from the squadron but continued the mission.

"I've got that call before," he told Chuck, "and it wasn't good news. We don't have to hurry back." They took aim at the target and kept on flying.

When they returned to base, Fig was back in the squadron when the Thunderbirds called again. He was surprised that Lieutenant Colonel Roger Parrish had tried to reach him. Previously a wingman had given him the news.

As he picked up the receiver, Newton heard, "Fig, this is Roger Parrish. Congratulations! You are a member of the 1975 Thunderbirds Team!"

Fig walked out of his office wearing a Very Big Grin! The folks in his squadron were thrilled for him. They had been pulling for his success. His selection was an honor for him and for his squadron.

Captain Lloyd W. "Fig" Newton, *your* USAF Thunderbirds Precision Flying Team was a dream no longer. *Yes*!

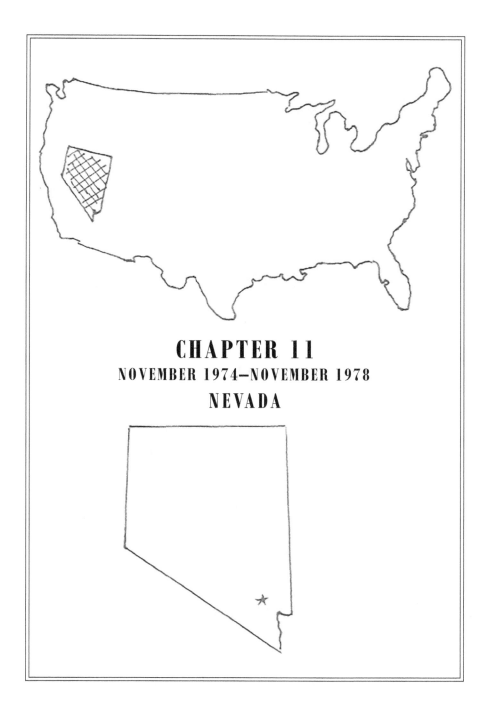

CHAPTER 11
NOVEMBER 1974–NOVEMBER 1978
NEVADA

*T*he United States Air Force became a separate branch of the armed forces in 1947. In 1953, at the height of the Korean War, Air Force Headquarters in Washington, DC ordered the formation of an aerial demonstration team to highlight the capabilities of front-line fighter planes and their pilots.

Luke AFB outside Phoenix, Arizona was chosen as the team's home base. The F-84, the "workhorse" fighter of Korea, and its squadron members were stationed there. It would be the aircraft of that first team. Colonel Levi Chase picked Major Smokey Catledge as the founding Commander/Leader. Catledge would be responsible for everything: finding pilots, crew, aircraft, housing, public relations, the name, paint schemes, aerial choreography—everything.

The official name was the 3600ᵗʰ USAF Air Demonstration Unit/ Flight, and its first code name was "Stardusters." After only three weeks, that was changed to the "Thunderbirds" in honor of the strong Native American culture in the Southwest where the team was stationed.

As Major Catledge turned to walk out of Colonel Chase's office upon learning of his new assignment, the colonel casually mentioned, "By the way, your first show is in three weeks."[22]

One week after *the* call, Newton was at Nellis AFB, Nevada, just outside Las Vegas. It was a "Magic Moment." One day, he was a captain in the squadron at Luke AFB, inspecting aircraft, instructing and doing paperwork. "In the blink of an eye, I'm now a captain in the US Air Force Thunderbirds," he said.

As a member of the 1975 team, he was Lloyd "Fig" Newton, #7 and Narrator. He and his crew chief, tall, redheaded Staff Sergeant Ray Herder from Brainerd, Minnesota, traveled everywhere together. It was Herder's job to inspect and take care of Newton's aircraft. He was also responsible for the setup of all the ground equipment at each airshow location, *and* he did all the paperwork. Teammates included the new leader, Major Chris Patterakis; Captain Gil Mook, left wing;

Captain Steve Mish, right wing; Major Doug Roach, slot; Captain Jim Simons, solo; and Major Ray White, logistics officer.

In '74, the team switched to T-38s rather than F-4s. The nationwide fuel crisis caused long lines of cars that snaked all the way around the block just to fill up with gas. The rationed days on which a driver could even get in those lines were determined by the car's odd and even last numbers on the license plate. The F-4 carried 6,000 pounds of fuel for a performance. The lighter, smaller T-38 required only 2,400 pounds. The switch was a smart choice, environmentally and financially.

As narrator, Fig would face the audience from the announcer's stand. With a stationery microphone, he would read the descriptions of the action overhead from a script. At the beginning of the '75 season, new leader Patterakis suggested they change it up a little by adding music to the airshow and narration. This was the first time in US military aerial-demonstration history that pairing music and flight motion had been tried. Getting the script to coordinate with the music and then getting them both to coordinate with the action while not even looking overhead at what was happening? Fig practiced and practiced with the team to get the timing just right.

One day during mid-season, Chris came over to Fig and said, "Why don't you put the book down and just tell the people the story? It will still be there for backup."

Soon afterward, during a Las Vegas airshow dress rehearsal, a civilian entertainer gave him a pep talk that he never forgot. "They don't know what you're gonna say or what you're supposed to say. You control the audience."

Whew! After those two changes, no script, and no pressure, Newton relaxed. Suddenly Fig's love of flying and rapport with a crowd filled his spontaneous narratives. The crowds loved the new format and the magic of a master storyteller. Because he had not made the team on his first two tries, Newton has always felt his eventual success was almost "spiritual." The airman realized of the prior attempts: "It just wasn't my time. Lord. You know best."

Flying with the 1976 team was quite an honor. As part of the United States' bicentennial celebration, commemorative logos were painted on the T-38s' tails along with a minor revised paint scheme on the fuselage. That year the team was scheduled for 110 air shows and performed 104 of them. The six cancellations were due to weather. This was an historic year for America and an historic schedule for the Thunderbirds. That was the largest number of shows they had ever attempted in a single year, approximately 65 being the current annual average.

Breaking the team's racial barrier as a pilot received a lot of media attention. The Air Force submitted an article to *Ebony* magazine about their new African-American Thunderbird pilot. In the spring of '75, the magazine staff called for more information before it published a four-page article on Jasper County's native son. Brother Marion called to tell him that the family had bought up every copy they could find!

For the 1976 season, Fig moved up to the #4 position, the Slot. As soon as the planes took off, the slot pilot, from about twenty feet above the ground, would quickly move over into the tight position at the rear of the formation. He would then tuck his plane in the middle of the other planes. On Fig's first flight, he remembers telling Major Doug Roach, "You're kidding me! I am *not* doing that!"

For three years, John and Annie's middle son traveled the country performing aerobatics in the sky. As the official Thunderbird narrator, he spoke to hundreds of thousands of people, telling his sky story. As the slot pilot, he would squeeze a 12,500-pound aircraft into a formation in which the planes were only four to six feet apart as they flew together at speeds of 400 to 500 mph.

While overseas, Lloyd Newton had learned about true humility and what it meant to those around him. When he arrived on the Thunderbird team, he had made a promise to himself: "This *won't* go to my head. I want people to think of me as the same Capt. Fig Newton when I leave this team as I was when I came on the team." He put that promise to work during all those hours of audience interaction. Around the country, the audiences were very accepting of the first black T-bird Pilot. The team received their warmest welcome ever in the middle of a cornfield in Ottumwa, Iowa. A team member looked around and teased Fig, "Well, here we are in the heartland of American black culture." Everybody got a big laugh as the pilots exchanged knowing smiles of appreciation for the camaraderie within their group.

Toward the end of 1977 and the last part of his Thunderbird tour, Fig received his next assignment from the Air Force Personnel Center. It would be a brief, temporary job but an important one for his future. He was being sent to the Armed Forces Staff College in Norfolk, Virginia to study the principles and techniques for joint-forces operations. Members of all branches of the service would learn how to effectively work as a team. Staff College was reserved for mid-level officers like the new Major Lloyd Newton.

Those five months in Virginia were definitely a tough decompression time. Fig switched from flying one of the toughest positions on the Air Force's most prestigious aerobatic team to returning to the classroom with books, assignments, and homework. He became grounded quickly in more ways than one. But he was getting more… well, you *know*!

In May, two weeks before graduation, student Newton received a call from Lt. Col. Joe Prater, former Thunderbird #6 and logistics officer. "Hey, Newton, how would you like to go back and fly with the Thunderbirds?" Prater asked.

"You're trying to jerk my chain," Fig joked back.

"No. Boss Cherry (Lt Col. Dan Cherry) called. Walt Parker needs an operation on his right arm, and Boss Cherry wants you to fill in." Prater told Fig to call Major General Billy Ellis for details. Fig knew he would miss the last few days of his Staff College experience. He wasn't even sure he would be released to go back to the team. *Well, if it has to be done!* he thought, trying unsuccessfully to suppress a grin.

But what about Ruby and the children? He had been gone a tremendous amount of time over the past three years. Although she and the three little ones had been in Las Vegas during his Thunderbird tour, everyone was happy to be back together. How would he break the news?

Fig sat down at dinner. After gathering his courage, he began, "Well, we have a little bit of a problem. The Thunderbirds called and…" When Fig finished his explanation, Ruby's reaction was "I think that's great!" The family had moved to Norfolk when he came east to study. Since this Thunderbird assignment would only be four-to-six-weeks of temporary duty, they decided to go stay with family in Ridgeland while he was away. As things turned out, Commander Cherry kept Newton on the team throughout the remainder of the 1978 season. Flexibility was all part of being a military family.

Later on, Fig's AFSC classmates would joke that he had graduated first in his class. They were referring, of course, to the chronology of the finish, not to the class ranking. He was just the first student to leave!

The political protests at home were subsiding. Performing from the East Coast to the West Coast and, especially in Middle America, Fig saw that this country was going to be okay. As with past troubles, most Americans would continue to work toward a better future for their children and grandchildren.

The public's respect for symbols of society, especially symbols of service, never failed to amaze him. The team was constantly barraged for autographs when in their flight suits or uniforms. As the first African-American member, sometimes Fig got more requests than the others. Fig couldn't help but notice an immediate difference, however, when they changed into their civilian clothes; almost no one recognized them.

"It's not about you, Newton!" he told himself. It was about that USAF uniform.

Getting an autograph let the public become part of the bigger picture represented by the Thunderbird pilots. Fig couldn't stop the flashback—little Lloyd at home in Ridgeland looking up to see Army Sgt. Major Lee Newton's uniform walking in the door. He knew from his own experience as a boy what his current uniform represented, especially to the young people around him.

Back at Nellis after the five-month Staff College detour, Major Newton flew the right wing position for three months while Walt Parker recovered. Then Boss Cherry made some additional changes on the team and asked Fig to stay on as narrator for the rest of the year.

So faded the crescendo of Fig's Thunderbird life. This had always been his *real* goal. How fortunate he had been to experience it in so many ways over such an extended period of time! Whatever else was asked of him, he felt would represent "pay-back time." He would gladly serve through whatever came.

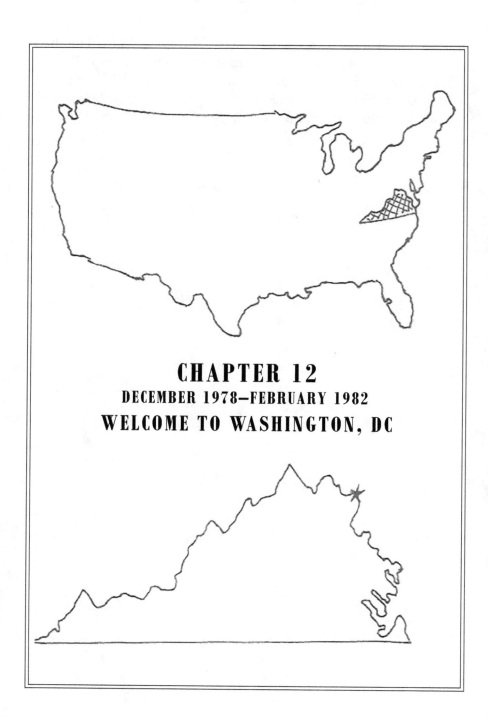

CHAPTER 12
DECEMBER 1978–FEBRUARY 1982
WELCOME TO WASHINGTON, DC

In December 1978, with his 36th birthday just around the corner, former T-Bird pilot Newton headed to Washington, DC. From a tough but treasured childhood in the segregated South, he had graduated from an outstanding black university, become a USAF fighter pilot, returned home a Vietnam War veteran, served as a jet-fighter flight instructor, and represented the Air Force across the United States and Canada on their official aerobatic demonstration team. His next assignment would require him to draw on the skills gained from each of these experiences, and then some.

The good old '66 LeMans had been retired to South Carolina when the family moved to the Philippines. Fig and Ruby gave it to her dad, Marion Gadson. Fig was now driving a family-friendly Volvo ordered directly from Sweden. It too would be in service for years. It too would eventually retire to Jasper County—in John's driveway.

Driving across the country on his 2,500-mile trip from Nevada to DC, Newton was probably wondering whether this new assignment was a "good birthday present" or one he would want to exchange. From the hot seat of a T-Bird T-38, he was moving to the hot bed of American politics—the Congress of the United States. As Congressional Liaison Officer for the Air Force, Fig would be working closely with members of the US House of Representatives.

He had tried to delay reporting to DC until after the New Year, but his superiors wanted him in Washington during the busy Christmas season. He would be able to meet people more quickly at holiday functions. Plus, everyone could get to know the new guy on the block. Having been a Thunderbird was always a good icebreaker.

Fig spent the first four months at the Pentagon where each branch of the armed forces had its own block of offices. He became adroit at navigating the corridors in those early days. The Major had another important mentor during this transition. His boss, Colonel Ted Rees, guided Lloyd through the world of joint cooperation among the branches of service.

He should have expected the response he got from his South Carolina family that April 1979 day when he told them he was calling from his new office...in the Sam Rayburn Congressional Office Building on Capitol Hill. "You're kidding me!" they exclaimed.

He worked with military officers of much higher rank on the leading edge of world movements. Happenings around the world related to many of the activities in the offices near where Newton now worked. He had almost daily interface with members of Congress and their staffs. The "South Carolina country boy," as he often thought of himself, was seeing his school days' history lessons come to life. While his career had taken him many places, this tour was the most broadening experience he had ever had.

His Capitol Hill job expanded his understanding of the USAF's role in the total international defense picture. In military environments, the generals were in charge, but from his Congressional Liaison desk, he was learning the civilian leadership reality. Who is truly in control? A Congressman filled him in with "Look, Fig, we're the ones that control the military." Newton got it. Funding! The money and the decisions as to where it would go were coming from Congress and, ultimately, from who he always knew he was serving—the People.

Although he was away from his jets, Fig's daily pace often felt just as fast. "I might have missed flying, but I have no regrets about giving it up for this assignment." Traveling was still part of the job. Most of the time he would dress as a civilian rather than in uniform when accompanying Congressional delegations abroad. The wardrobe was all about first impressions. A group of US Congressmen and their staff walking into a room of diplomats on foreign soil *with an escort in military uniform* projected a much different statement than the same group entering the negotiations room *in suits and ties.* Each detail in international situations required careful consideration at every turn.

The trips were government-to-government meetings. Arrangements were made through the US embassy staff with the host country. Upon arrival in a country, the delegation would report to the Embassy to meet with the current Ambassador or senior embassy staff member. All American embassies are guarded by the US Marine Corps. The Marine on duty was the first contact-person when the delegation drove up. Major Newton, career Air Force officer, always felt proud. Those soldiers were sharp in their uniform, their presence, and their protocol. "Meeting our Marines all over the world made me so proud to be an American. It's really cool! Really terrific!" Fig exclaims.

Major Newton was a member of two diplomatic missions of global significance during his time in Washington. The first was to China and the other to South Africa:

China is the third largest country in landmass in the world, about half the size of Russia. It has two major geographic areas. Tibet-Xinjiang-Inner Mongolia is in the north and west. Its mountains, high plateaus, and basins are home to steppes and uninhabitable deserts. In contrast, China Proper's mountains, hills, lowland plains, and lowlands are densely populated, and its land has been continuously farmed for centuries. Two of the world's longest rivers run through the country. The Huang He (Yellow River) is about 2,900 miles long. Because of its unpredictable flooding and turbulence, no major cities skirt its banks. The Yangtze River has a 3,400-mile-long course along which much of China lives.[23]

China was a land ruled by ancient dynasties for millennia, dating back before 2500 BC, followed by a period of ever-changing rulers from warring provinces. Beginning in 200 BC until the beginning of the 20th century AD, imperial dynasties reigned. For centuries, it was a country of mystery, yet it was known for many firsts in invention, industry, and technology. Its rulers preferred, even demanded, isolation from the outside world. The Polo family of Venice, including the explorer, Marco, established trade routes into China in the second half of the 13th century. Thus the imperial gates were opened to the rest of Asia and Europe.[24]

The Xinhai Revolution of 1911 overthrew China's last imperial dynasty and established the Republic of China. Mao Tse-tung, a Communist Revolutionary, founded the People's Republic of China in 1949, ruling until his death in 1976.

In his later years, Mao agreed to an historic meeting with United States Secretary of State Henry Kissinger. Their talks began the process of normal-

izing diplomatic relations between the two countries. In 1972, President Richard Nixon became the first American president to visit Mao and the People's Republic. He "opened" 20th century China to the western world.[25]

China had amazingly reopened diplomatic relations with the West. Newton traveled with Congressional Majority Leader Jim Wright (Texas) and his entourage as Wright's military escort on one of six agreed-upon trips to Mainland China. His previous experiences in the Far East, along with his knowledge of Asian cultures were important assets when working on the logistics of this breakthrough conference. Being one of the first westerners to officially visit the People's Republic of China after the recent United States-China normalization talks was a once-in-a-lifetime opportunity. He received an introduction to Chinese culture while witnessing a major global political change.

The semiarid country of South Africa is at the southernmost tip of the African continent. Its geography divides it into three sections—narrow, fertile, and tropical coastal valleys; interior semiarid plateaus; and the mountainous semiarid Great Escarpment. Despite the overall lack of water, the land is filled with great biodiversity of plants and animals.[26]

The native San people ruled the land when Dutch settlers arrived in 1651. With the 1756 import of slaves, the Boers (Dutch) established a white-minority-dominated rule called "apartheid." Great Britain took control in 1815, and South Africa gained its independence in 1908. The new government, however, chose to maintain the apartheid rule of the past even though black Africans made up 80 percent of the population. The black majority then founded the African National Congress (ANC) in 1912 to fight this oppression. The conflict between these two political factions dominated the 20th century.

Apartheid laws became increasingly restrictive—grossly limiting and unfairly regulating every aspect of black life. International anti-apartheid pressure began in earnest in the 1960s following the 1963 imprisonment of the ANC resistance leader, Nelson Mandela. In the 1970s, South African blacks and whites joined in protest against international companies doing business with the apartheid government. Worldwide pressure for boycotts of these companies gained strength throughout the 1980s. This was economically devastating to South Africa. Finally, the white government had no choice but to consider the beginnings of change.[27]

In 1981, another US Congressional Delegation led by Majority Leader Jim Wright and including Freshman Representative William Gray (Pennsylvania), Colonel Rees, an NCO, and Major Newton traveled to South Africa. The policy of apartheid had created critical times in the divided South African nation. The separation of the races was as severe to the black population as if they lived on reservations. Nelson Mandela was still held in a Johannesburg prison on Robben Island off the coast of Cape Town.

Many US corporations were doing business with South Africa. The international calls for boycotts of these companies and the American people's disapproval of the country's apartheid culture made it increasingly important for the US government to become involved in a solution. Still strengthening its own civil rights progress at home, the United States had no desire to support a country that continued such human disrespect.

The area around Johannesburg reminded Fig of Vietnam. Its beautifully tropical physical geography stood in sharp contrast to its harsh political geography. Yet here he was in Africa, coming to assist in improving human rights, just as he had done in the Philippines, Vietnam, and other countries.

In 1978 Desmond Tutu was appointed General Secretary of the South African Council of Churches and became a leading spokesperson for the rights of black South Africans. During the 1980s he played an unrivaled role in drawing national and international attention to the iniquities of apartheid, and in 1984 he won the Nobel Prize for Peace for his efforts.[28]

The delegation's first meeting with newly appointed Desmond Tutu was in the district of Soweto while his church was still under curfew. The limitations of enforced segregation were not extended to the US delegation and its black military escort. Newton was treated with colorblind equality, as long as he was in the secured areas with the other US travelers.

One night, Fig was invited by some black South Africans to travel from Johannesburg back to Soweto for a private party. Since the two locations were only about an hour apart, Fig accepted. The time passed by quickly. The people, the discussions, and the music were great. Fig was certainly enjoying the evening. Suddenly the entire group realized it was past the 11:00 p.m. curfew for black citizens. How were they going to get back to Johannesburg? Everyone in the group was black except for one white Englishman.

Someone said, "Just stay the night." But Fig hadn't told *anyone* in the congressional group where he was going or what he was doing. He hadn't even checked it out with his superior officer, Colonel Ted Rees. *Not* a wise decision, he has since always admitted!

They hurried to their vehicle. As soon as they pulled outside the fence surrounding Soweto, a car started following them. About fifteen minutes down the road, the car sped up and passed. It was easy for those in the passing car to see the black driver of Fig's car (an embassy driver). At a checkpoint twenty minutes down the road, bright lights flooded their vehicle. Soldiers with automatic weapons surrounded them. All four doors were pulled open. "Get out!" they were ordered. The security personnel searched them and the car very thoroughly. Fig had done one thing right that night. (In fact, he sometimes remembers it as about the smartest thing he ever did.) He had made sure to have his US passport in his pocket. When the soldiers saw it, they left him alone. Meanwhile, the embassy driver received a thirty-to-forty minute grilling.

Standing there at that checkpoint, Fig's nerves were as tight as when he was in Vietnam or during race riots back home. Just like years ago when he had to tell his parents about his North Carolina traffic accident, he was now even more worried about having to tell his boss what had happened. He was humiliated that Col. Rees might have to get him out of a South African jail.

Finally they were allowed to proceed. The remainder of the trip was spent in total silence. When they got back to the hotel, he didn't put it off. He went right to Col Rees with his story early the next morning. And what a story it was!

The big pay-off for the heavy Washington, DC workload was monumental. At the end of his first year of this three-year assignment, the Air Force must have thought he was doing a pretty good job. He was promoted to lieutenant colonel. He had gone from Jasper County to China. He had accompanied members of Congress to meetings with the Saudi Arabian Crown Prince during a period of heightened Israeli-Arab tensions. He had witnessed world conferences where international leaders negotiated policy. These were extraordinary opportunities for both personal and professional growth.

As his congressional liaison tour came to a close, he remembered that he was, after all, a pilot. He was feeling the "need for speed." MacDill AFB would remedy that. In February 1982, he headed for Tampa, Florida. He had loved the challenges of Washington, but he was ready to trade them for the chance to climb up into that new F-16 Fighting Falcon.

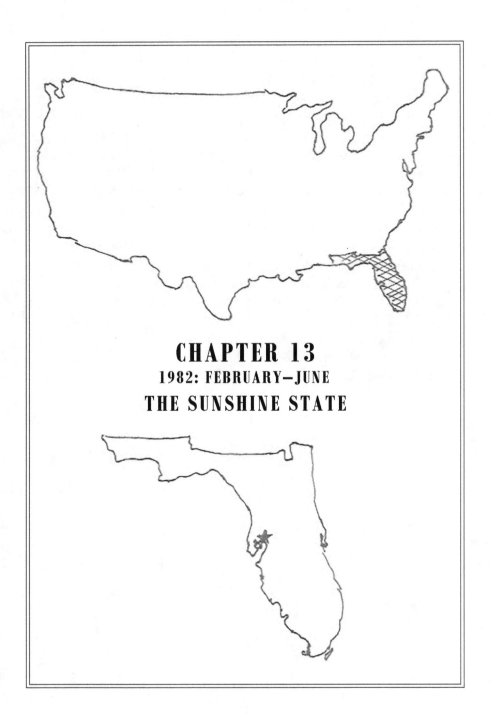

CHAPTER 13
1982: FEBRUARY–JUNE
THE SUNSHINE STATE

Lt. Col. Newton was so happy when he found out he had been transferred to MacDill that he wanted to pay the Air Force! It was snowing, and the temperature was in the thirties as he drove out of Washington, DC. When he stopped over in Jasper County, he spent time with as many friends and family as possible. He especially loved his time with John and Annie, catching up and just being together across the table. Hopping back on I-95, the weather was much better now. He smiled at the blue skies of Florida as he pulled into a Jacksonville car wash to get rid of the dried snow and dirt that reminded him of cold DC. A few hours later, he arrived in Tampa. As he drove along Bayshore Boulevard with its beautiful sidewalk balustrade, he gazed across Tampa Bay searching for sight of the Air Force base at the tip of the peninsula.

He knew this would be a short transitional training assignment. For that reason, the family decided to remain in the DC area for the duration. Fig thought back to another transition a few years before. In those five months back in 1977 at the end of his official Thunderbird tours, he had exchanged the best-of-the-best kind of flying for a seat in an Armed Forces Staff College classroom. This time, MacDill AFB was taking him away from a desk that had anchored him for almost three years to the newest high-performance aircraft.

The first time he climbed into the F-16, Fig "felt like I was sitting out on the end of a pole or in the nose of a rocket." His familiar F-4 Phantom seat was much lower in the fuselage. With the higher seat and bubble canopy of his new ride, Newton realized he couldn't see the nose of the aircraft. More new changes would be all about the "tech." This new-generation, post-Vietnam aircraft mirrored the next era of technology. Fig was a bit nervous about all the surrounding newness. After talking with the MacDill Base Commander, however, he got some reassurance.

"Everything you need, I'll get you," the Commander said. "But I can't study or do the flying for you."

The Commander was right. The pilot knew he could learn important lessons from everyone. What Fig saw and had to learn about on the panels, in the jet's design, and in its increased capabilities took this lesson in K-N-O-W to a whole new level.

Not only was he being upgraded as a pilot, Lt. Col. Newton was also being prepped to become a squadron commander or a higher position in the 8th Tactical Fighter Wing, Kunsan Air Base, South Korea. Several of his MacDill classmates would also be heading there with him.

Fig had to admit that every bit of the knowledge he had learned at the Armed Forces Staff College about joint-forces coordination had been used almost daily during his Congressional Liaison duty. Now he was returning to the Far East. How would these latest experiences be put into play in his upcoming South Korea years?

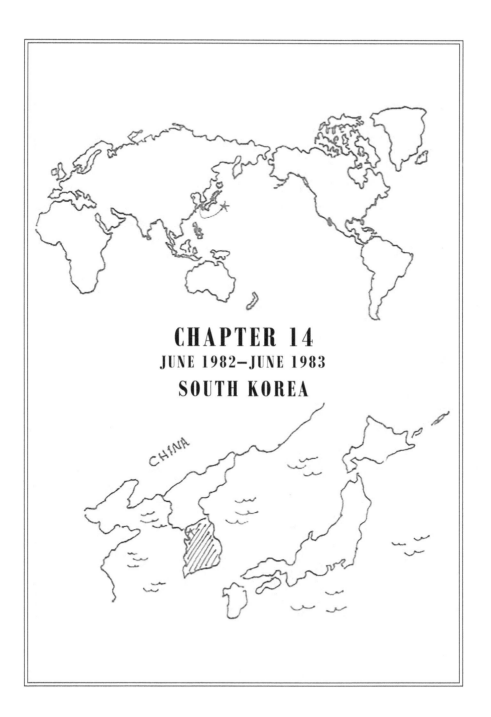

CHAPTER 14
JUNE 1982–JUNE 1983
SOUTH KOREA

CHINA

Fig made a quick trip back to Virginia to say goodbye to Ruby, Lloyd Jr., Cheryl, and Lori before heading for South Korea. Ruby had started her own floral design business. That and single parenting kept her busy! The children were in familiar schools with friends close by. That made Dad's absence easier for them. Classified as a remote assignment, no families were allowed at Kunsan Air Base, which is about a hundred miles south of the Demilitarized Zone (DMZ). Fig would be alone in Korea.

The Korean peninsula reaches southward into the Pacific Ocean from Mainland China. Still north of that lies Russia. Across the East China Sea is its eastern neighbor, Japan. The peninsula's mountains are almost everywhere. Most other countries along the Pacific Rim are subject to the upheavals of the "Ring of Fire." Korea, though, is unusually stable geologically, with no active volcanoes and only rare earthquake shocks (although a 5.1 earthquake occurred off the coast of South Korea in February 2014).

Its location, sandwiched between two historic empires, resulted in Chinese and Japanese domination over the centuries. Following World War II, it was divided into two independent countries—North Korea, under communist influence, and South Korea, industrialized and western in philosophy. In 1950, the North tried to invade and annex its southern neighbor. The Allies, led by US military, provided support to thwart the action, known as the Korean War. A tenacious truce was set in place in 1953, but the political tensions have never subsided. The 38th Parallel agreement, based on that 38th line of northern latitude, established a land buffer between the two countries. It is called the Demilitarized Zone (DMZ) (no troops), but there has been and remains continued allied military peace-keeping forces stationed right at its edge.[29]

As Lt. Col. Newton headed for Kunsan Air Base, he thought about the day he had left the Republic of the Philippines nine years before. He looked forward to his return to another Pacific-Asian republic. The base was about eighty miles south of the capital city, Seoul, and about a hundred miles from the DMZ. A second Allied air base, Osan, was just outside Seoul. It was close enough to North Korea to remain in a state of constant alert, with thousands of troops between Seoul and the DMZ. An invasion from the North could happen at any time. Readiness was paramount.

Once in Korea, Newton's status was in limbo. Before leaving the States, Fig was informed by his Commander, Col. Paul McManus, that he was selected to be on the full colonel promotion list. Because of his new rank, this meant he couldn't be a squadron commander as he had planned. He also knew he would be spending a lot of time in a cockpit, but he wasn't sure what his specific job would be. He signed in at the 80th Tactical Fighter Squadron and secured his flying gear.

Soon afterward, Fig got a call to report to the Wing Commander, Colonel Jim Record. They had met briefly at MacDill a few weeks earlier. "You need more F-16 experience," he began. This requirement of extra flight time didn't come with a specific title nor was it part of any job description. Col. Record's orders were clear: "Just go fly!" Fig remembers those two months as "pure flying pleasure," extraordinary in both scope and training style. The pilots were placed in combat-like roles without actually being in conflict. Fig compared these months of air training to the US Navy's "Top Gun" naval aviator training. Unlike the navy program, however, the F-16 training was tight with camaraderie without the intense competition.

Two months later, Jim Record called Fig into his office for another conference. "Guess you thought we forgot about you," he began this time. Newton soon found out he had definitely not been forgotten. He would now be assigned as the Assistant Deputy Commander of Operations for the entire Kunsan Air Base. His new boss, Col. Mike Rhodes, would become his leader, mentor, teacher, and fellow fighter pilot. Their friendship continues still today.

The two were taking a truck ride from the office to the BOQ (Bachelor Officer Quarters) when Mike dropped a surprise announcement: "Well, the full colonels' list is out, and you are on it." While this was not a total surprise, Fig was relieved to officially hear that he had been selected.

This was news of the double-edged sword variety. The rank of full colonel was a tremendous recognition and career move for Newton. It came, however, with a tradition of hosting a big celebration party for the whole base—all at the expense of the base's new colonels. Fig asked Rhodes how many others were on the Kunsan list because they would all share the expenses. The colonel looked over at Fig with a sheepish smile and said, "Just you." The party was great! The base personnel were introduced to a new leader, and the new colonel was reminded that he was responsible for a *lot* of airmen of all ranks.

In his new position, Fig worked closely with the South Korean Air Force and national government. His years as a Congressional Liaison paid extensive dividends. In his travels with United States/South Korean delegations and in his interface with South Korea Air Force leadership, his skills in negotiations and international protocol continued to advance.

Fig respected the Korean people just as he had the Filipino culture. They worked hard and were gracious and friendly. They remembered the Korean War conflict and the support they had received from the United States, and they welcomed the continued American military presence below the 38th Parallel.

Sometimes, Newton laments, some American "bad apples" did not return that respect, embarrassing themselves and their nation with their behavior. They would lose sight of the Golden Rule, acting out with an arrogance of affluence.

One Saturday morning when Fig was going shopping, he was at a bus stop. Both Korean civilians and US off-duty military stood waiting. The young Americans started harassing a group of Korean teens. Just as the two factions squared off, Fig stepped right in between them. Turning to his countrymen, he demanded, "Why are you doing this? They weren't bothering you." Things broke up. He had received an awful lot of experience in healing cultural clashes both at home and on foreign bases throughout his career. He hoped this time a positive lesson would be carried home.

Two flying wings shared Kunsan Air Base—American F-16s and South Korean Air Force F-86s. The "86s" were older fighters meticulously maintained by the Korean airmen and their crews. Today the Koreans also fly F-16s.

Everywhere one looked, the South Korean countryside was covered with young trees, almost all planted in the 1970s. These forests replaced those destroyed during the 1950s war. It was not until the 1970s, however, that this struggling nation could afford such a massive environmental reforestation. Nothing escapes war's devastation. The Koreans came back from that destruction, however, with grit and determination. With scarce funds and limited resources, they rebuilt their infrastructure (roads, bridges, shipyards, utilities, etc.). That framework supported reconstruction and restoration of buildings and homes. The international city of Seoul was clean, modern, efficient, and productive.

Learning from their past, the Koreans' new road system was built in preparation for potential future conflicts. They knew they were located in a strategically precarious location. The main roads have no medians or concrete barriers. They have built-in runways and are striped for use as emergency landing sites, if needed. There are drilled piling holes, ready for poles to be placed for traffic control. A plane could land, refuel, and takeoff. Then traffic could resume.

The Koreans utilized every acre of land on this small peninsular in innovative ways. Their economic situation in the 1950s was similar to the US Great Depression of the 1930s. Both countries had remembered what they *didn't* have during those times. When recovery began, Korea rethought, preplanned, and retooled for a more efficient future.

One clear day, Newton was part of an F-16 four-ship, training flight over a mountainous region. The lead plane had received the wrong navigation data in its computer navigation system. When the pilot realized that the data was wrong, he tried to insert a correction. It was too late. His low altitude position left no time for escape. The aircraft crashed into the mountainside, killing the pilot. The loss of a pilot is a very tough experience. Something like that, even for trained fighter pilots, never gets easy.

In mid-December of 1982, a Marine F-4 Phantom squadron out of Beaufort, South Carolina had flown over to Korea for combat training with the Air Force F-16s. One day during maneuvers, Marine Squadron Commander Randy Brinkley's F-4 was involved in a head-on wing-to-wing crash with an F-16 over the Yellow Sea northwest of the South Korean peninsula. The damaged F-16 headed toward land. The pilot ejected and landed on the beach. Despite his exposure to the brutal December wind and near-freezing temperatures, he was okay and was recovered shortly thereafter.

Brinkley's F-4 Phantom had lost part of its right wing. Fighting for control, he flew back to Kunsan Air Base. With the aerodynamics of the wing crucial for creating enough lift for landing, the Marine tried twice to come down safely. Twice he failed. He then radioed the control tower that he was heading out over the water for a controlled ejection. He was now thinking of the safety of everyone on base as well as that of the planes and base facilities in the area.

Col. Newton was the Supervisor of Flying Officer that day, and he got on the radio. In no uncertain terms, he ordered, "Randy, you are *not* going to eject into the water. Come back around and put that thing on the ground." Fig knew the few minutes of survival time in the extreme Yellow Sea winter environment would not be long enough for a successful rescue.

The Kunsan runway was cleared and prepared for the in-coming emergency aircraft. Fig knew the F-4 Phantom's capabilities, and he knew the qualified pilot in command. The plane screamed down out of the sky. The drag chute was deployed as it touched down and raced to the end of the runway with tires on fire. When Brinkley finally stopped the aircraft, he and his back-seater jumped out of the plane as military firemen foamed the aircraft and the area. They were safely on the ground, and no one was hurt. The plane was saved, and no rescue was required.

Being the Marines that they were, the South Carolina squadron maintenance crew towed the plane back to the hangar. They went to work the best way they could with whatever they could find. A good example of their ingenuity: a Pepsi Cola can was just the right size to plug one of the holes on the tail of the aircraft. Three weeks later, the plane flew out again. Marines can, indeed, fix anything.

Fig was second in command under Col. Mike Rhodes for the operations of the base aircraft. Two important events coincided during this time that Fig won't easily forget. The Inspector General of the US Pacific Air Forces announced an upcoming official inspection. Simultaneously the F-16 squadron was planning to deploy to Australia. Not a bad duty location, Fig mused. How was this going to work? Boss Rhodes had it all planned. He left for Down Under with the squadron, and Fig remained at Kunsan to greet the Inspector General and his team. "Mike ran off and left me," teases Newton.

As fate would have it, then-Brigadier General Dan Cherry, Fig's former Thunderbird team leader, was the leader of the IG team. While they were glad to see one another, their friendship did not influence the professional expectations of the inspection. Both Cherry and Newton understood: "It's nothing personal. It's just business and that's the way it is." The mission always comes first. Adhering to that priority strengthens friendships while simultaneously maintaining the highest military standards. Fig was extremely proud of his unit's teammates. They passed the inspection with flying colors, which was no real surprise to Brigadier General Cherry.

Remote tours normally last one year. The military realizes that one short year is still a long twelve months for personnel and family alike. The first place Fig flew that June 1983 after bidding Korea goodbye was to Washington, DC to re-unite with his family. That's when he gave them the news: Hill AFB, located between Ogden and Salt Lake City in northern Utah, would be the next stop.

Lloyd in 5th grade, 1954.

Lloyd in his Explorer's Boy Scout uniform, 1958.

Fig with classmate John Allen at the gun range in pilot training, 1967.

Fig and former wife Ruby during pilot training graduation, 1967.

Fig ready to fly combat mission at Da
Nang AB, South Vietnam, 1968.

Fig's first year with the Thunderbirds and as the Team Narrator, 1975

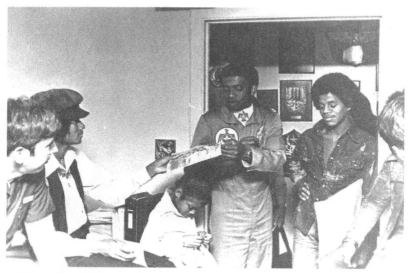

Fig with members of the "The Jackson Five" singing group, 1975.

Fig signing autographs after an airshow, 1975.

Fig with his crew chief, Wayne Jackson and their
parents & with Wayne's son, 1976.

Fig and his brother Captain Lester Newton, USAF C-130 pilot, 1976

Fig and Elouise just married, with their Matron of Honor & Best
Man, Mindy & Ray Bean. Vance AFB, OK, January 1989.

Fig with his high school teachers, Ms. Georgia
Caldwell (l) & Mrs. Ollie McAlister (r) 1992.

Fig at Holloman AFB, NM
before going to fly the F-117
Stealth Fighter, 1993.

Fig with President Bush, AF Secretary Shelia Widnall and former CSAF, General Ret. Tony McPeak, 1997.

Fig and Elouise with his Mom, Annie and her mom, Ida Mae at Randolph AFB, TX, 1997.

Fig and Elouise with General Ron Fogleman, CSAF, during Fig's 4th star promotion ceremony. March 1997

Fig and Elouise with family and friends after his 4th star promotion, Randolph AFB, TX 1997.

Fig getting ready to fly F-15 Eagle, 1998.

Fig visiting with students at a Space Camp, 1998.

Fig and Elouise with Brigadier General Ret. Chuck Yeager,
first person to fly faster than the speed of sound. 1999

Fig with David Robinson of the
San Antonio Spurs, 1999.

Fig with Four Star General (Ret) Jacob Smart, both served in the Air Force and both are from Ridgeland, SC, 2000.

Fig passing the flag to General Michael Ryan, CSAF, during
Fig's retirement at Randolph, AFB, TX, 2000.

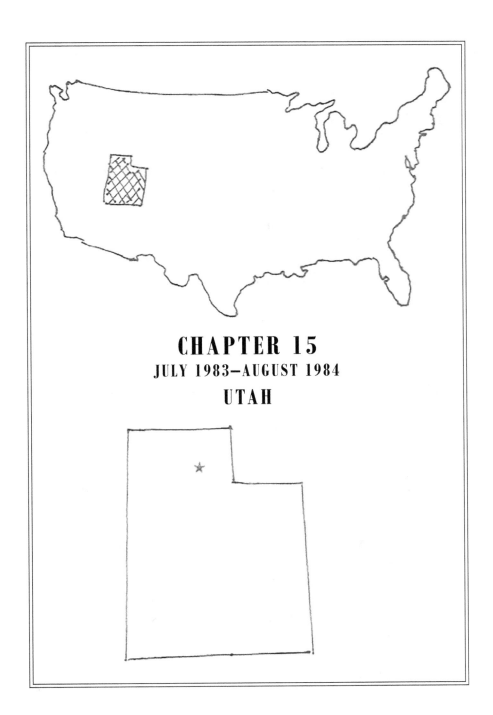

CHAPTER 15
JULY 1983–AUGUST 1984
UTAH

Fig enjoyed his month with Ruby and the kids. Too soon, it was time for him to head to Utah. With many assignments lasting a year or less and with other tours requiring constant travel, he and Ruby were committed to giving their children a stable home environment by staying in one place. This meant Fig missed out on a lot of his children's growing-up experiences and the majority of the parenting responsibilities fell on Ruby's shoulders. Had they moved more often as a family, Lloyd, Cheryl, and Lori would have been in different schools with different friends every year or two. Fig had the camaraderie of his fellow airmen. Ruby had her business associates. The children had their school and neighborhood friends. But each had a piece missing as they all served the nation in their own special "ranks."

July 3, 1983, Colonel Newton reported to Hill Air Force Base, Ogden, Utah, home of three squadrons of F-16s. As Assistant Director of Operations, Fig reported to Col. Kent Bankus. Prior to his arrival, Col. Bankus had mentioned, "By the way, we're having a Fourth of July picnic the day after you arrive. It would be a good idea for you to attend. It will give you a chance to meet everyone." So in those first few days and at the picnic, Fig met many of the personable military and civilian families with whom he would work in the upcoming year.

"Hello. You must be Col. Newton," Fig heard as he walked into his new office for the first time. "My name is Jean Webb. I'm filling in for my sister, Judy. We share this job." Job sharing was a new concept in the early 1980s, and Hill AFB was one of the first places to help it succeed. Fig would become a big proponent of that system, both while in Utah and with future opportunities.

At the beginning of the next week, Fig walked into his office. "Hi, I'm Judy Lemon." This time he wasn't surprised but pleased to meet the second half of his competent administrative team.

Being stationed stateside didn't mean he was through traveling. For Ocean Venture '84, a joint Air Force and Army air and ground training exercise, Senior Officer Newton and one squadron were deployed to San Juan, Puerto Rico. Upon his return, both Jean and Judy brought an Ops (Operations) truck to pick up the boss. Driving up to the office building, Fig noticed some people standing around outside. The girls couldn't help themselves, and they started laughing. Soon Fig understood why. *Someone* had moved his entire office outside under a big tree! "It was a crazy ride with Jean and Judy," Fig recalls. "There was never a dull moment." Jean, Judy, and the Newtons remain close friends, still calling often to check in.

Ocean Venture '84 holds a couple of other special memories for Fig. Prior to deploying, the colonel and other officers flew to Bergstrom AFB near Austin, Texas for a planning meeting with the Commander, 12th Air Force. While in the restaurant at Austin International Airport awaiting their flight back to Utah, Fig saw some money on the terminal floor—three $100 bills! He remembered who had been sitting there just about five minutes before. Fig and the officer traveling with him went searching for the strangers who were just getting into a cab. How very, very thankful they were to have their money returned and to meet two people whose integrity made it possible!

A few weeks later, in Puerto Rico, Fig was out to dinner with the same officer who had been with him in Austin. As they headed back to base, Fig discovered that he had lost his wallet. Returning to the restaurant, he was relieved to learn that the manager had found it. He returned it to the colonel, totally intact.

The officer who had witnessed both "lost money/lost wallet" episodes commented, "Fig, you're getting blessings back!" Fig totally agreed!

Not all the memories from Utah were good ones. One morning shortly after returning from Ocean Venture, Fig was already in his office about 4:00 a.m. The phone rang.

"Sir, come to the Command Post. An emergency beeper is going off."

That meant a possible aircraft crash. While practicing intercepts using radar at approximately 25,000 feet, a pilot had seen a distant train light in the dark mountains. He thought it was a star. Disoriented, the pilot flew toward the light and into the ground of the pitch-dark desert.

Later, two separate F-16s were lost while practicing over the gunnery range. One was during the winter snows when the horizon disappears. As a result of the three accidents, Jim Record (Fig's commander in Korea) was brought in from Luke AFB to take over. It was terribly difficult for everybody on the base to lose those pilots and then to have their wing commander, their "coach," fired. As a result of the changes, Judy was moved over to work for "Commander Record," breaking up the tag-team Jean-Judy act. Folks adjusted. They graciously welcomed the new commander into that tough situation. All persevered.

"Much of my own leadership style I learned from Jim Record. He was a great officer, leader, and an important mentor for me," Fig praises.

With his Utah hourglass almost empty, Fig knew he would remain grateful to the Utah civilians, almost all of the Mormon faith, who had helped him throughout the year. They were fantastic people, hard workers, and true friends with impeccable ethics. He had also grown to love the high desert mountains and plateaus of the area. Why, he had even learned to snow ski!

Back in Virginia, Lloyd Jr. was now in high school and driving! Cheryl and Lori were doing well with their academics, and Ruby's business was flourishing. They were all glad that Fig's next tour would return him home. He would be going to school again but this time in DC.

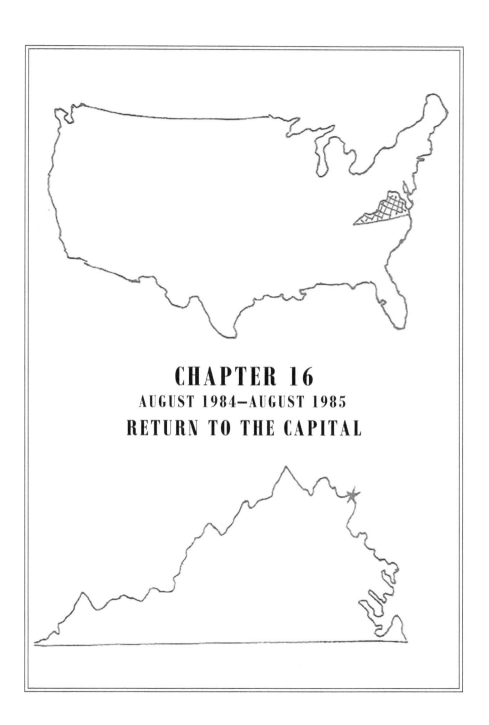

CHAPTER 16
AUGUST 1984–AUGUST 1985
RETURN TO THE CAPITAL

Fig used his August leave time to catch up with the kids and Ruby. This homecoming, however, was a little more restrained and... strained than ones in the past. The years of being apart for long periods of time had slowly taken their toll on the Newtons' marriage. Both adults had grown apart in their professional lives and in their emotional relationship. Ruby loved flowers and had made a success of her floral business. Fig continued to develop his career and serve the Air Force. They decided to separate and later divorced. However, they remained totally committed to their children who would always come first.

As September approached, it was time for that great American tradition—back to school. This year, there would be *four* Newton students heading to the classroom. New student, Fig, now had two important jobs—helping his teenagers adjust to their parents' separation and attending the National Defense University (NDU) on Ft. McNair, Washington, DC. A lot was going on in his heart and his head.

Like all universities, NDU has several colleges, the most well-known being the National War College. Unlike more familiar public and private schools, however, the National Defense University does not take applications from interested students. Every member of its student body has been carefully chosen by one of the five branches of the armed forces, US government civilian agencies, and allied nations. Upon being selected, the students don't get "acceptance letters" like the ones high school seniors stay up nights hoping for; instead, the new NDU students receive a copy of the school's selection list and their *orders* telling them when and where to report for class.

From September 1984 through May 1985, Fig attended the Industrial College of the Armed Forces. The Ft. McNair campus was both beautiful and stimulating. It was close to Lloyd, Cheryl, and Lori, too. While he missed the flying, Fig enjoyed the opportunity to further his education. The courses covered topics as broad as International Relationships and Diplomacy, Principles of War, and Logistics of War. This training was essential for any senior military leader of a world power. In his classes he met officers from all branches of the US military, employees of other departments of the US government, and international officers working for Allies of the United States. It was a joint-coalition environment of military and civilian students.

In partnership with NDU, the private, civilian George Washington University offered GW courses on the military campus. Professors from George Washington came there to teach classes. The colonel dual-enrolled for a GW master's degree. The business and public administration curriculum was particularly rewarding. He realized this coalition-style learning created a direct link between civilian thinking and military policy development.

Newton had seen a glimpse of this system during his Congressional Liaison years. In the Philippines and Korea, he had worked with both foreign military leaders and the civilian leadership. The blended academics were preparing him for future successful civilian partnerships. He now had a greater understanding of how to use all the knowledge.

In April, just before his May graduation, Fig was on a trip to Japan with the Industrial College. During a meeting with a Japanese electronics company, the colonel was told he had a message from the States. It was a message about his younger brother, Lester. He was an Air Force lieutenant colonel stationed at Ft. Eustis, Virginia, but he was flying out of Langley AFB, Virginia. He had been a passenger on a T-39 flight to Wilkes-Barre, Pennsylvania, with the Commander of Tactical Air Command, General Jerome O'Malley, his wife, an instructor pilot, and their crew chief. Lester was to copilot the plane back to Virginia after dropping off the Commander and his wife.

Upon landing in Wilkes-Barre, the brakes malfunctioned. The pilot attempted to abort the landing and get airborne again, but he wasn't able to get enough altitude. The plane struck some trees. His brother and all the others were killed.

Lloyd and youngest brother Donald wore their uniforms as the six siblings joined Annie and John for the memorial service at

Langley AFB, Virginia. Lester's death hit Lloyd hard. They were back-to-back brothers. They had always been close. They were both Air Force pilots. A couple of years later, Fig felt that he really *needed* to visit the site of the crash, to say a final goodbye and try to get some closure. He called the Wilkes-Barre airport to get permission. On a Saturday, an airport fireman took him to the crash site and left him for a while. There he paused and sought peace.

Fig graduated from the Industrial College in May, but his Master's Degree in Public Administration coursework from George Washington University was not finished until August 1985. Thus, he remained a full-time student on campus for three more months. This kept him close to his teenagers throughout that summer, allowing them to have more time together.

Fig continued to take Lloyd Jr., Cheryl, and Lori to see both sets of their Ridgeland families during holidays and vacations. Those ten-hour drives from Alexandria, Virginia to "The Farm," as the Newton family called their South Carolina homestead, were great trips.

Fig remembers how Cheryl would be first to claim a backseat because she always wanted to bring a lot of friends...of the stuffed-animal-and-doll variety. Dad found it necessary to set a three-friend limit. But Cheryl, a *non*-uniformed daughter, not an airman under the Officer's command, would adjust his orders by hiding extra animals and dolls in the car before they left. As for Lloyd Jr. and Lori? Well, they just vied for "shot gun."

Divorce is never easy for the adults or for the children involved. The five Newtons worked through it each in their own way.

Thinking back over his career thus far, Fig had always kept an optimistic "glass half full" attitude. He sometimes felt he had never had a "real job" because his entire career had been so rewarding! He had just completed another full year of higher education: John Newton was more and more pleased with his son's increasing *know*ledge!

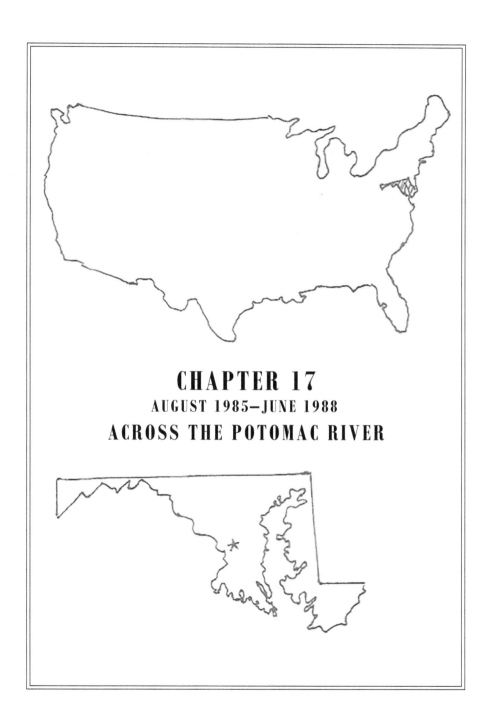

CHAPTER 17
AUGUST 1985–JUNE 1988
ACROSS THE POTOMAC RIVER

T he graduate's new assignment was right across the Potomac River in the basement of the Pentagon. Col. Newton was now Assistant Deputy Director for Operations and Training. His office was at the headquarters for the US Air Force.

His new superior officer, Col. Stanley O. Smith, had flown B-52s. Once again, as when he trained for Vietnam, Fig, the fighter pilot, was working closely with a bomber pilot. Col. Smith told him right away that in the Office of Operations he would sometimes have a prominent impact on the Air Force and the country, yet at other times, he would be making absolutely no impact. The key would be to learn the difference and act accordingly.

Secondly, Newton was reminded that he didn't know big planes. He was ordered to Minot AFB, North Dakota, to get some firsthand knowledge of bomber aircraft and strategic forces.

His first lesson began after landing. It was October, and it was already snowing in Minot! During the pre-flight briefing for a B-52 refueling training mission, Fig noticed some smirking from the guys around him when he was told he would get a chance to air refuel the B-52. He didn't pay it too much attention. What did they know that he didn't?

The next day, the training flight began. The copilot flew in the left seat (pilot-in-command position) during takeoff for the first part of the mission. The refueling KC-135 tanker had taken off first. The B-52, with Fig, the copilot, the flight instructor, and the crew flew to the designated practice area. There they followed a type of oval-race-track-in-the-sky flight pattern. Fig noticed the copilot having some difficulty positioning the bomber into the refueling position. "How hard could it be?" he wondered, having refueled his fighter aircraft many times before.

After nearly an hour of observation, Fig was called to try his hand at flying the big beast. With his fighter refueling experience, he was used to a control move of approximately three inches maximum to connect with the KC-135 refueling probe. However, the B-52 behemoth had eight throttles versus just one on the familiar F-16. He wrestled with the maneuver for thirty-five minutes and never got it into the refueling position.

There were major differences between the two types of aircraft regarding aligning the refueling probe. Those three inches of "wiggle room" while maneuvering a tight, small fighter were proportionally skies apart from the same space with a massive bomber. The crew-members had known ahead of time just how tough it was; that was the reason for their smug grins during briefing. Now Fig knew it, too! Looking back on his first F-4 refueling experience in 1967 at George AFB, California, all he could think was *What a difference! It wasn't anything like that B-52!*

Back at the Pentagon, the fighter pilot humbly admitted to the bomber commander, "Now I know what you meant about learning something about big planes."

By 1986, Colonel Newton's career had taken him halfway around the world and back more than once. He had spent twenty-two of his forty-four years, half a lifetime, serving his country.

His new assignment kept him at the Pentagon. Now he would be Director of Special Projects, serving under the Directorate of Plans. "Special Projects?" What did that mean? He would find out. Major General Dugan approached Col. Newton regarding a classified job working for Major General Al Logan. As part of the briefing for this new assignment, a staff member projected a photograph of a unique aircraft onto a screen for Col. Newton to observe.

"Sir, do you know what this is?" he was asked.

"No, I don't," Fig replied.

"Sir, this is the F-117A Stealth Fighter."

"When are we gonna build that one?" Fig asked.

With a smile, the briefer replied, "Sir, we've already got two squadrons, and you are going to go see them."

There were three deeply classified aspects to this assignment— the B-2 Stealth Bomber, the F-22 Fighter and the F-117 Nighthawk Stealth Fighter. None of these projects was public knowledge. All had code names. The major and two lieutenant colonels briefed him. The new Director of Special Projects was learning about one of the most special Air Force projects to come along in quite a while!

The F-117 squadrons were secretly based in Nevada. The pilots were publicly stationed at Nellis AFB, Las Vegas. They officially flew A-7s and T-38s. Yes, they really did fly these planes but only out to Tonopah Air Base, a smaller facility in the Nevada desert. Here their real jobs began. They were the combat pilots for a new-age jet that was stealth (invisible) to radar. They would fly mostly at night. The jets remained hangared most of the time as protection from Soviet and other spy satellites. The project was stealth in radar invisibility and stealth in its existence. Not only did the public not know, but neither did the families of the Tonopah personnel. For all those classified years, the spouses and children could not be told where or what their family members were up to.

Some of the United States' closest allies were briefed on the Stealth program. Once during a visit by President Ronald Reagan to the United Kingdom, Prime Minister Margaret Thatcher made it known to the president that she would like to have a RAF (Royal Air Force) pilot assigned to the Stealth program.

The Commander in Chief called the Pentagon, and Fig's folks were given an order to make it happen. Just before the Gulf War, a British RAF officer joined the stealth fighter squadron. Keeping key Allies engaged has been important throughout our history.

Fig loved nothing better than having family members visit. At the time, one of his young nieces, Vanessa, had moved up to the DC area from South Carolina. It was early '86, and Fig's staff had been working long hours for two-plus weeks on a special Pentagon project. On a late February Friday, as a break from their hard work, he had invited his project teammates and Vanessa to join him at Andrews Air Force Base Officers' Club.

Arriving at the club, still in uniform, he and Vanessa noticed his staff in the lounge area. A good friend, Sharon, with whom Fig had worked on Capitol Hill, happened to be there too. She saw him and came over to say hello. A great rock and roll band was playing to a lively crowd on the dance floor. He told Vanessa he would be right back.

Afterwards, Fig walked Sharon back to her table. He noticed someone there who he hadn't seen before. How did this young woman happen to be at the Officers' Club? Sharon, a civilian, was dating an Air Force guy. Her date worked at Systems Command in the office with the person not yet known to Fig.

Sharon, a big fan of Fig's, introduced him to the lady with "I want you to meet my good friend, Fig Newton."

"Hi, I'm Elouise Morning," came her reply.

Fig asked if he could join them. Soon, though, he remembered that he had left Vanessa at the bar with his staff members and all those young, single officers. Even though she could take care of herself, he thought it would be a good idea to check on her. Excusing himself, he touched base and then rejoined Sharon, Elouise, and another friend, Cindy.

After Fig had done this a couple times, Elouise became suspicious. "Who is this niece you keep going to check on?"

Fig caught on that Elouise thought he was visiting another lady friend, not a family member. Accepting the challenge, he answered, "Oh, would you like to meet my niece?" And he left to bring her right over. "Meet my niece, Vanessa." To Elouise's surprise (and perhaps, relief), the young girl really was *family*.

The conversation with Ms. Morning went well. They even danced a few times. What Fig didn't know at the time was that as he left the table to check on Vanessa, Elouise had said to Cindy, "What grown man would call himself Fig Newton?" She didn't yet appreciate how important Fig's nickname had become to him and his career.

The band stopped playing, but Fig and Elouise kept talking. The bartender made a last call announcement, and everyone at the table began to walk out. Fig and designated driver, Vanessa, walked Elouise to the front sidewalk of the club. There he told Elouise that he had enjoyed the evening and that he would be in touch.

As Fig and Vanessa started to walk away, Elouise turned and asked, "How are you going to contact me? You don't even have my number."

Fig replied, "Oh, I'll get it!"

As she watched the two Newtons walk across the parking lot, Elouise thought to herself, *How arrogant!*

Fig knew, though, that he would call Sharon and ask her to find Elouise's number. When he called to ask, his friend didn't disappoint. During the middle of the following week, Fig called Ms. Morning. They met for dinner. This was the beginning.

As Elouise and Fig learned more about each other, they found they had a lot in common. Elouise was a former Air Force spouse as well. They liked to do the same kind of things—theater, the movies (Elouise was a big movie fan!), and traveling. They both loved seafood, and they enjoyed just being together.

One common topic often discussed was that of being a single parent. Fig's three children and Elouise's two sons had all been through the divorces of their parents. All the children made adjustments they had struggled through. The two new friends did also.

"It was definitely something we could talk about," Fig remembers.

The colonel added one more important K-N-O-W experience to his resume while serving at the Pentagon. He was selected to attend a six-week National Security Senior Executives Course at Harvard University in Cambridge, Massachusetts. From Jasper County to the Ivy League! All of these opportunities gave Fig important new skills for his life and his work.

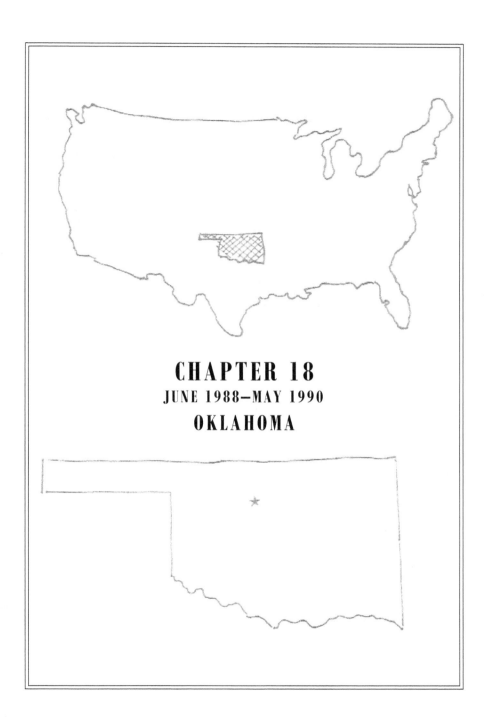

CHAPTER 18
JUNE 1988–MAY 1990
OKLAHOMA

The couple had been dating for almost two years when in early June 1988, Elouise received the devastating phone call. Her younger son, James, now a high school senior, had been in a terrible car accident. James was in Dover, Delaware with his father and had been struck by a drunk driver while backing out of a driveway. She rushed to Dover to be with him and found that he had sustained a spinal cord injury. He was transferred to Philadelphia for surgery where he remained for several weeks followed by an airlift to the Texas Institute of Rehabilitation and Research (TIRR) in Houston, Texas. Their world had been turned upside down.

In July 1988, after five stable years in the Washington, DC area, Colonel Newton received some surprising news. He had a new assignment. On that July morning, the personnel officer said, "Congratulations, Sir. You are going to be the Base Commander at Vance Air Force Base, Enid, Oklahoma."

Base Commander? That was quite a shock! Fig was expecting to go back to flying F-16s again or at least some type of fighter aircraft. What self-respecting fighter pilot wanted to be grounded behind a desk, commander of "roads and commodes" while jets soared overhead? And in...Enid, Oklahoma?

Let's see about this, he thought.

As soon as he walked into Gen. Al Logan's office, the General began laughing and said, "I knew I would see you after you heard the news. They need you, Newton. You're the right guy."

Not willing to give up yet, Fig asked permission to speak with Lt. Gen. Mike Dougan who was in the next level of command. "Permission granted," Logan responded, and off he went to the General's office.

"Oh yeah, they need you, Fig," was General Dougan's reply.

Newton was suddenly filled with self-doubt. *Why do they want me there? Is it because I'm divorced now?* he wondered to himself. What about his children? How could he leave Elouise at this critical time?

How would she handle their separation? Would she even have time for him with the urgency of James's situation dominating her every moment?

He reached out to a good friend, Dick Toliver, for a sympathetic ear. Fig was "crying in his milk" about Vance AFB having no fighters, only trainers; he would be the Base Commander, and on and on.

After he stopped complaining, Dick turned to him and said, "Fig, the Lord wants you in Enid, Oklahoma."

A few weeks after his counseling session with Toliver, he began the long drive westward to the Sooner State. The further he drove along I-40, the more conflict swirled in his head. He was leaving the headquarters of the USAF, the center of action, and he was leaving his children and Elouise. He remembered having these same feelings when he had wanted to return to Vietnam. Then he remembered all he had accomplished when he was sent to the Philippines instead.

"Okay, Lord. What's this all about?"

What's that old saying, "Ask and you shall receive"? It didn't take long for an answer.

Fig had gone a little farther down the highway when he pulled over to chat with a guy on a combine in a wheat field. Here they were, just two farmers talking farming. Memories of the Carolina fields, heat, and sweat-soaked shirts came rushing back to him. Thinking about his roots helped to calm him down. Farmers usually have to come up with their own answers when problems arise. And there was his answer! He would use both his low-country skills and all those degrees of new K-N-O-W-ledge for whatever Vance AFB problems he encountered.

His new decision: "I'm going to be the *best* Base Commander they've ever had!"

Reporting to base, Newton quickly settled into his assigned housing. Commanders are required to live on base for security and accessibility. He met his superior officer and then got to know his team of airmen and civilians. They would be one of the best groups of employees with whom he ever worked. Yes, it was tough to leave Washington, DC, but he found that he had definitely underestimated the people of Oklahoma as well as the job satisfaction he would get from this position. That key change in attitude back on the road was already paying dividends. He is still grateful for the staff that taught him the ropes in his first base commander's job.

Vance AFB was one of five pilot-training bases. Uniquely, though, most of the operational work there was handled by a civilian contractor, Northrop Corporation. That included facilities, aircraft maintenance, civil engineering, construction, and base operations. The military handled the actual flight instruction and management. This efficient partnership was a somewhat new arrangement then; however, today it is used on many bases worldwide. Fig, with the help of the civilian contractor, was managing the logistics for basically a small city. In addition, Fig had the responsibility of meeting and greeting every new class of pilot trainees, all those new second lieutenants, who came to train at Vance AFB for flight training. It was a rewarding responsibility.

Elouise's son had been transferred to Houston, and Fig had gone to Oklahoma. The only thing that made sense to her now was to take a leave of absence from her job in DC so that she could be in Texas with James and be a part of his rehabilitation. This was her new fulltime job.

She and Fig talked often, and he visited from Vance as much as possible. Trying to help her remain upbeat, one day, he decided to ask his on-base next-door neighbors, Wing Commander Ron Shamblin and his wife Mary Lynn, to give Elouise a call. As soon as Colonel Shamblin got on the line, he began by telling her that "the guy next door (Fig) was having wild parties every night" and that "there were women and wine every time I looked over there!" Fortunately, Mary Lynn grabbed the receiver and saved the day by explaining her husband's sense of humor.

"Yeah, he got me really good," Fig laughingly recalls.

By the time a few months had passed, Newton loved Oklahoma and its people. He could see the results of his work—upgrading the maintenance on the base and on the trainers. Bob Lyons, a retired colonel and F-105 pilot, taught him all he needed to know about the facilities. Everywhere he looked, he found good counsel.

Elouise came to Enid for a couple of weeks in December 1988. It was great to be together again. He enjoyed introducing her to his new friends. Her warm personality and charming wit endeared her to everyone. Fig felt more and more indebted to Sharon for that Officers' Club introduction a couple of years before. The holiday season and his Christmas Eve birthday were pretty great that year.

As the couple grew closer, they would talk about not wanting to make the same mistakes in a new relationship that they had experienced in the past.

They both concluded that they could not be specific about what they wanted in a new marriage, but they were very sure about what they did not want. Their most important commitment was "to be thoughtful with spoken words, especially during a disagreement. Once words have been spoken, there is no amount of "I'm sorry" that can make you unhear what you've heard. They continue to hold true to that commitment today.

"Never say anything that you don't really mean, especially when angry. You can't make 'old' friends. Once you lose them, it's over," Fig advises. That's true in marriage, in friendships, and with family. Be ever mindful (Appendix IV).

After New Year's Day, on the first Wednesday of 1989, Fig turned to Elouise and said, "I'm going to marry you."

"Yeah, right! When?" came her feisty retort.

"Tomorrow."

"Sure! You're kidding!" she replied incredulously.

"No, I'm serious." And with that, Colonel Newton, drawing on his southern-gentleman background, officially proposed.

As it turned out, because of the official paperwork, it took two days instead of one to prepare for the wedding. Fig had forgotten that they needed a marriage license. On Thursday, they headed downtown for the legal paperwork. The couple had always planned to have a small, simple wedding.

When Fig arrived at the office on Friday morning, people began congratulating him. *How did they know?* he thought. Because it was a matter of public record, their license application had been published in the local paper. He also wondered why his office door was closed and people around him were whispering.

Fig called his deputy commander in with a "What is going on, Jim?"

"Sir, we're not going to do anything to embarrass you, but you can't drive yourselves to your own wedding."

After that, Fig walked around inviting key friends and staff to the ceremony that evening. He also made sure Commander and Mrs. Shamblin received a personal invitation. They asked Colonel Ray Bean and his wife Mindy, a couple that they had met while stationed in DC and was now the Assistant Deputy of Operations at Vance to be their best man and matron of honor.

That Friday evening, January 6, 1989, Elouise M. Morning of St. Petersburg, Florida and Lloyd W. Newton of Ridgeland, South Carolina were married. The Base Chaplain presided over the ceremony. The small chapel was still decorated for Christmas as they walked in to the music of Lionel Richie's "Jesus Is Love." They were surprised to see the pews filled with many more guests than they had expected. After the ceremony, the newly married couple came back down the aisle to the music of Willie Nelson's "Blue Skies."

With only short notice, Fig's staff had gone into high gear and created a memorable occasion for the new couple using the discipline and organization that is part of military life. Plans included an Air Force Honor Guard forming the traditional military crossed-sword arch through which they descended the chapel steps. Colonel and Mrs. Newton then left the chapel in a shower of rice amidst a clamor of cans tied to the back of their car. A beautiful private reception was held at their new home.

This was the beginning of a new phase of their lives as parents of a blended family of five, committed to God, country, and family. Elouise moved into the official base commander's house. As both a former Air Force spouse and employee, she understood that she could contribute most by being true to the person that she was. She embraced her new role as Commander's wife and the responsibilities it included. Now an "Air Force couple," Col. and Mrs. Newton would work together for the good of the people of Vance and its mission.

After five short months, Fig got a call from the Air Education and Training Commander.

"How would you like to be a wing commander?" the general asked.

"Sir, I'd love it!" Fig answered, but he simultaneously thought to himself how much he really liked the job he was doing.

The general continued, "How about the wing right there at Vance?"

So in April 1989, Fig had another flying job. As wing commander, he would be flying the T-38 trainer. Now, how was he going to tell his bride the news? She was about to learn just how quickly the military could turn things upside-down. Elouise was thrilled when she heard of his new command after such a short time. He then told her about one of the benefits of his new position. While Fig would move to a new office, they would also need to move to a new house—the official Wing Commander's residence. Elouise laughed because that move was only about fifty yards away to the house next door. This was their first official Air Force move.

James had been released from rehab in Texas and was now with them in Oklahoma. Elouise worked hard to help him adjust to the new norm both at home and in the new high school. She remembers: "We were lucky enough to have two high school seniors living on both sides of us. They embraced James and made his transition much easier. The community was also very supportive which allowed him to remain the easy-going person he had always been, making lots of friends even as the new kid."

They enjoyed that second home for a full year. Then it was time to pack again. The irony was not lost on Fig. As hard as it had been for him to move to Oklahoma, when they prepared to leave, he had to admit that this, of all assignments thus far, was perhaps the toughest goodbye of his career. It was there they married and began their lives together. Vance Air Force Base and the local Enid community had been a very special place. Elouise and Fig explain that "the community embraced our family, and we love them for every act of kindness shown us. They will always be a part of who we are."

The two began their drive south to their next home—Randolph Air Force Base in San Antonio, Texas. Along the way, they talked about their plans to explore the Texas hill country and to enjoy San Antonio's River Walk.

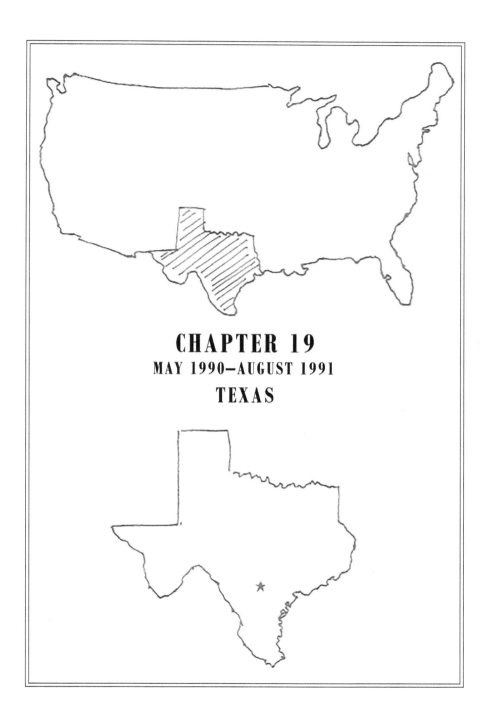

CHAPTER 19
MAY 1990–AUGUST 1991
TEXAS

Colonel Newton left Vance AFB as commander of the 71st Flying Training Wing. He arrived at Randolph AFB as Commander of the 12th Flying Training Wing. Somehow, someway, he had moved from one state to another, from one assignment to another, yet he was still in the cockpit. The T-38 trainers would continue to be this "bird colonel's" wings.

The couple was amazed at this opportunity. They had learned about the move before the official notification when General Bob Delligatti stopped at Vance on a trip from Randolph. He casually mentioned, "By the way, you're going to Randolph."

"Sir," said Fig, "you mean—"

"Oh, yes! General Bob Oaks will be giving you a call." When Fig arrived home and filled Elouise in on the news, he still couldn't believe it.

"Really? Me?"

In a few short weeks, the call came from Gen. Oaks. "Fig, we're gonna bring you down to Randolph." The official comment was spoken.

Fig was as excited as a kid on a Jasper County Christmas morning. Randolph was one of the premiere bases in Air Education and Training Command in the entire Air Force. Plus, he would *still* be flying!

Before Texas fought and earned its independence from Mexico and before it gave up that independence to become the twenty-eighth state in the United States of America, its vast land had been home to many indigenous peoples. They left remnants of their culture to be discovered. As the northern part of Mexico, many Spanish and Mexican settlers later lived there. They, too, left traces of their lives on the Lone Star landscape.

The architecture at Randolph reflected this long Texas heritage. The beautiful on-base home into which the Newtons moved was built in the Spanish style. So was the Officers' Club, set in the middle of the base. Fig's office building, complete with a Spanish-style tower, was dubbed the Taj Mahal. His was a pedestrian lifestyle. He enjoyed the ability to walk wherever on base he needed to be.

His main assignment was two-fold—training of instructor pilots and management of whole-base responsibilities. Both the Navy and Air Force aeronautical navigation-training centers were at Randolph. The Air Force's Personnel Center was there also. Colonel Newton had a multitude of programs around him.

The United States military loves Texas and Texas loves the military. The San Antonio area alone was home to five military bases. These facilities provided a large percentage of the economic impact and employment of the area. One of the highlights of the community was the San Antonio Fiesta held each April. The "first-class" Mardi-Gras-style festival was a wonderful experience for both locals and thousands of military personnel away from home. Each individual base hosted activities during the festival season. This added to the excitement and the local culture. It was a welcome break for Elouise and Fig and for the servicemen and women in the area.

In expected military style, leadership rotated out while Newton was at Randolph. General Oaks, with whom Newton had worked so closely and effectively, was sent to Europe. The new Commander, General Joe Ashy, arrived with a new style and new expectations. Here again, the Colonel's attitude about life—doing the very best he could and learning as much as he could (K-N-O-W)—stood him in good stead. General Ashy was a tough commander who planned big changes. Being known as a great fixer of bases, even one as good as Randolph, it was no surprise that he wanted to change out the "old" and bring in the "new."

"You never get a second chance to make a first impression." Fig recalled that initial day with the new Commander. It was a tough one! He could not seem to do anything fast enough or good enough right from the start. Fig headed home feeling pretty beat up but still holding to his "do my best" philosophy.

The next morning when Newton reported to work, his phone rang. General Ashy was on the line. Fig was surprised to hear the General's voice. Ashy had seen what work was needed on the infrastructure of the 1930s-built base and in a "command" tone, he told

Fig that he wanted to get the base fixed. He then asked, "How much money do you need to bring this base up to standards?" Together they planned repairs, demolitions, and reconstruction.

Following a busy two weeks, they met again, reassessing what had already been accomplished and set in motion thus far. The effort was large in both scope and expense; Fig was a bit concerned about the already rising costs. When the subject of money came up, Ashy looked squarely at Newton and commented, "You haven't spent that money yet?" With that, Fig knew his team would have whatever support was needed to do a top-notch job.

The war in Iraq, Desert Storm, began January 16, 1991, 7:00 p.m. (EST). General Ashy invited all the senior commanders on the base to his home to watch the unfolding events on television. One of the strategic planners of the attack was there also. (Unlike most of the country, this officer knew ahead of time how the battle would begin.) That military action has been called America's first true "media" war. Fig was there, watching it unfold.

At the onset of the Civil War in 1865, local residents came out to see some of the first battles, settling on hillsides with picnic baskets to watch the battlefield excitement. When the fighting began in earnest, however, reality demanded a hasty retreat. The same naïve reaction to early strikes in Iraq again could be felt—this time on television screens, on the reporters' faces, and in their voices. Once again Americans gathered to watch the beginning of a war. Once again most of them prayed.

Stateside, daily life and jobs continued. A few months later, Joe Ashy called Fig into his office again.

"I just got a call from General (four-star) Mike Loh at Tactical Air Command. He's gonna call you."

Fig knew it was time for his next assignment. He realized that having a single wing-command job in a career was a major accomplishment. As he was finishing his second such assignment, he looked over his career game board as he speculated: would he be heading to a staff job at Langley AFB, Virginia or back to the Pentagon?

During the months they served together, Commander Ashy and his "wing man, Newton," along with their wives, had developed a strong, long-lasting friendship. As had happened so many times before, their separation would prove to be bittersweet for both families.

For Fig Newton, Joe Ashy was tough but fair, and he acquired many valuable lessons under Ashy's command. Learning to lead confidently, manage fairly, and get tough things done in tough times honed Colonel Newton's abilities. He still feels today that without those Ashy-led challenges, "I would never have gotten my first star." General Ashy taught his staff to better discern what he wanted and how to deliver results. When the goals were accomplished, he would reward their hard work. He was "the only commander I ever worked for who gave me more money than I could spend to get the job done." What Fig realized was that, although the General had set very high expectations, he also came through with the resources to secure his team's success.

The Jasper County native looked forward to putting these newly acquired lessons to work at his upcoming assignment. Where would that be?

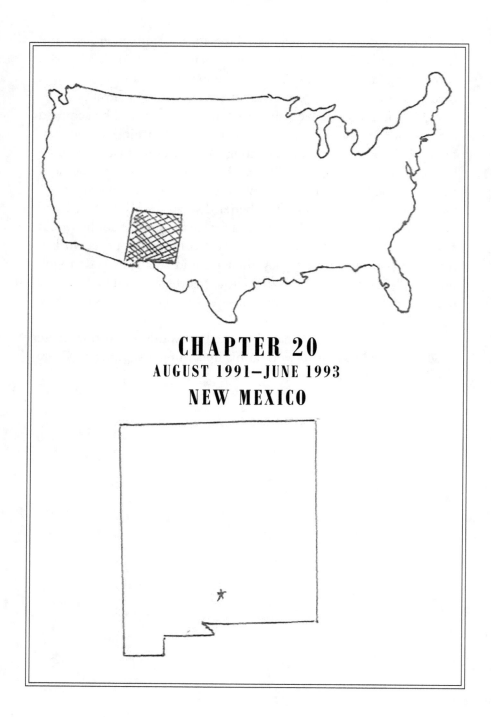

CHAPTER 20
AUGUST 1991–JUNE 1993
NEW MEXICO

W hen General Mike Loh felt the time was right, he gave Colonel Newton the call that he knew was coming, thanks to the tip-off from Joe Ashy. Loh got right to the point. "I have a very important job for you at Holloman AFB. I need someone who can handle this mission." Hearing the New Mexico location, Fig immediately thought, *What staff job would be at Holloman?* He knew there would be aircraft at Holloman, lots of aircraft! Yet he was already completing his second wing commander's job.

The General continued, "We're going to move the F-117 out of Tonopah and into the public at Holloman AFB."

Fig took a deep breath. Becoming the commander of the 833rd Air Division would be one huge challenge. Although the F-117 had been revealed to the American public, the base location was still not widely known. He would now have to handle the complete unveiling of one of the most renowned fighter aircraft in history. Little did he know back in 1986 when he saw those first photographs of the "Special Projects" stealth fighter that he would one day be the Commander of its Wing.

Would all that Fig had learned and all of his prior experiences be enough to help him through the upcoming preparations and media blitz the Stealth would bring with it to Holloman? Looking back on those glorious Thunderbird years, he knew he had developed an ability and passion for interacting with the public and the press. He had successful experience in those situations. He would dust off and polish up those skills for the new challenge ahead.

Prior to his departure from Randolph, Fig learned that he had been selected for the rank of Brigadier General. He would be joining the General Officers Corps.

A couple of months later in August 1991, General-select and Mrs. Newton began their two-day tandem trek. Driving their Saab and Camry, they used pre-cellphone walkie-talkies to keep in touch. The lush central Texas hill country gave way to flat west Texas range. It was a land populated by long horns and bobbing oil rigs. Leaving the El Paso plain, the black-green evergreens of mountainous eastern New Mexico gave a welcome reprieve from the Texas sagebrush. The arid high desert plateau of central New Mexico, however, quickly replaced the sweet scent of pine and fir. Fig knew they were getting closer as they sped toward Holloman.

They dropped down out of the mountains and continued on the long straight road. More barren mountains now filled the horizon. Elouise noticed that the large desert in front of them was brilliantly white and shimmering. "Welcome to the White Sands," she said to herself. As they approached their new hometown of Alamogordo, they both noticed a sign. "The Friendliest Place on Earth," it read.

"All right," crackled Fig's voice over the walkie-talkie. "We're going to be turning left onto the base just up ahead as we go under that overpass."

Elouise glanced all around from her driver's seat. Seeing nothing on the plateau but dunes upon dunes, the recent hill-country resident replied, "You mean this is it?" Fig couldn't help but think, *This may be a long two years!*

Elouise was also wondering what these next two years held for them. The citizens who had adopted that motto on the sign she had just passed would soon dispel her concerns.

New Mexico has always been known for its fascinating people and places. Ruins and other archeological evidence place indigenous peoples there 13,000 years ago. The pueblo culture of a thousand years ago continues today. Near Holloman AFB, their new home, the Newtons would find Carlsbad Caverns National Park. Every October, Albuquerque, the state capital, hosts thousands of hot air balloon pilots, crew, photographers, and visitors from around the world for its annual Balloon Fiesta. Roswell remains a recognized center for extraterrestrial enthusiasts. On a remote patch of parched land south of Albuquerque stands Trinity Site, the test site for the world's first nuclear explosion. The Newtons' new hometown of Alamogordo held a jewel of a surprise—the New Mexico Museum of Space History. Just outside their back door stretched the White Sands Desert, a geologic formation unique in the world. Yes, their new home's physical surroundings were sparse, even harsh, but they held their own type of beauty that nourished the rich culture carved from the land.[30]

Commanding Holloman Air Force Base's 833rd Air Division was a sweet assignment for any pilot, and it was at Holloman that Fig was awarded his first star. The prior lessons learned at Randolph would serve him well for what lay ahead. Already stationed there were F-15s and T-38s. His new orders included preparations for the arrival of the elite F-117. Holloman had neither shelter for the sensitive stealth skin of the valuable aircraft nor security for its cutting-edge technology. The desert heat, the scouring sand, and prying satellites needed to be repelled. A construction budget of $175 million was managed adeptly, with the final project coming in ahead of time and under budget.

How had Holloman and central New Mexico ended up with so many types of aircraft on one base? In the late 1980s and early 1990s, federal governmental consolidations and base closures were occurring throughout the world. This resulted in a squadron of German-owned F-4 Phantoms moving to Holloman. Fig knew that in two years, the wing of F-15s would be departing, leaving the F-117s and their companion T-38s secure in their new home. For the time being, however, he would be handling three different types of aircraft as he settled into the daily routines at Holloman.

In the midst of managing all the building preparations for the F-117, Fig was also planning how to handle the rush of the public, the politicians, and the press. Everyone would be asking for access to the stealth stars when they arrived. Yet as construction continued and plans progressed, another media flood was roiling toward the desert.

As he settled into the daily routines of Holloman, a few months after his arrival, Fig discovered a new debate had developed in America that was heightened by the Persian Gulf War and tensions in other parts of the world. It centered on the suitability of placing women in combat roles and, more specifically for the Air Force, in fighter cockpits.

The debate over inclusion of women in combat in the armed forces was a historic one. Women had gone undercover as male soldiers in the Revolutionary War. They have served in whatever roles were available in every US conflict. Women Airforce Service Pilots (WASP) and Women Army Corps (WAC) World War II pilots were critical to the success of the war effort. The planes would not have gotten to the front lines had it not been for them. The first female cadets arrived at the Air Force Academy in 1976. They were greeted by a sign reading "Bring Me Men." When the Academy commander was asked, "What are we going to do with this sign?" he quickly answered, "Well, you're gonna take it down!" Bringing women into any new military venue had almost always included tension.

Approximately six months earlier, the Air Force Chief of Staff, General Tony McPeak, had announced at a Pentagon press conference that the Air Force would indeed allow women in full combat situations. Simultaneously, he named Lt. Jean Marie "Jeannie" Flynn as an initial candidate for fighter training.

Just as he had helped facilitate racial equality and multi-cultural understanding in the ranks earlier in his career, it was only fitting that now in 1992, Newton was again steering his troops through the tumultuous current toward gender equity. When Lt. Jeannie Flynn, the Air Force's first and sole female fighter-pilot candidate (and first in US military history), arrived in Alamogordo with her male counterparts, the press came along too. The goal of the class was fighter pre-combat training in the T-38 that included lingo and maneuvers for an air-to-air or air-to-ground combat role.

Once again, Fig was shaking his head at the irony of this new situation. Yes, he was preparing for a Holloman press briefing, but no, it wasn't about the F-117. Here he was in the middle of even more pressure, from both the press and within the branches of the services, pertaining not to a new type of aircraft but a new type of pilot.

He laid out a plan for the news conference. First, he would address the media with opening remarks. The reporters' request for an interview with Flynn upon her arrival, he thought, was a reasonable one. Their desire to return every week or so to check on her progress, however, was over the line. This had never have been requested for male pilots, he noted. Lt. Flynn deserved and would receive the same treatment and the same respect as the other members of the class.

Newton planned to begin the press conference with his comments and give Lt. Flynn the opportunity to make initial remarks. He would then open the briefing to initial questions directed toward him. Finally, she would take the floor again to answer questions directed to her. He would remain on-stage to intervene if needed.

On the day of the press conference, things were going just as the Commander had planned. Question after question darted from the crowd. Jeannie stood before them confident, capable, and articulate in each response. Fig just smiled to himself and melted into the background. She was handling the podium the same way she would handle the cockpit—like a USAF fighter pilot.

Throughout her training, Lt. Flynn was treated and challenged just like any of her peers. The question had been posed to Fig at the press conference as to whether her training would be handled any different from the other pilots.

"Absolutely not," he shot back.

When addressing her male counterparts regarding his expectations of their behavior, he challenged them to "think of how you'd act if your sister was training here." Personally, he felt that Jeannie, like his own dear sister, Dorothy, would be able to handle anything that arose.

(Author's note: both then-Lt. Newton in the 1960s and Lt. Flynn in the 1990s, entered their new opportunities facing challenges on two fronts—in the curriculum and in the culture.)

Fig was really enjoying the runways in New Mexico. Right from the start, he was flying the T-38s and F-15s. When the German F-4s arrived, he logged hours in them as well. Prior to the arrival of the F-117 Nighthawks, the General flew to Tonopah Air Base, Nevada, where he was checked out in his new aircraft. By the end of his Holloman tour, he had flown all four aircraft. General Newton just loved his job!

The Commander reflected back on what he had learned about his new wing of F-117 fighters five years before when he was Director of Special Projects at the Pentagon:

- It was the first aircraft to exclusively use stealth technology, making it invisible to radar.
- Almost everything was stealth—its design, its technology, its flights and operations, its base location, its pilots, and its acknowledged "non-existence."
- It was based and tested in the Nevada desert at Tonopah Test Range Air Base.
- Its 4450th Tactical Group designation under which it served was officially located at Nellis AFB near Las Vegas.
- Its pilots officially flew the A-7 Corsair II out of Nellis AFB.
- Their real jobs—pushing the new aircraft through maneuvers and over mountains, mostly at night, the more moonless the better.

The new fighter had played a major role in the Persian Gulf War of 1991, Operation Desert Storm. It was the first aircraft to make a strike in the war. Its first target was to take out Iraqi President Saddam Hussein's military radar sites. Its mission was for ground attack, not aerial combat, but the name "stealth fighter" is how it will always be remembered. During Desert Storm, it received another title. The Saudis called it *Shaba*, the Arabic word for "Ghost."

Each of the 558 Air Force pilots who have flown the F-117 is known as "Bandit." The individual number following this moniker is assigned according to the chronology of each pilot assigned to fly the aircraft. General Fig Newton checked out on April 25, 1992. Thus as the 399th pilot to fly the aircraft, he became "Bandit #399."

This was the package that was being delivered to Holloman—a super-secret, very expensive, extremely effective aircraft that Fig would be responsible for keeping protected, even though it was now public knowledge.

By the arrival of the first F-117s in May 1992, temporary shelters awaited them while construction of the permanent hangars was well underway. The previous August, Fig had become the Commander of the 49th Fighter Wing, still at Holloman. This was the result of a reorganization of the Air Force's command structure and the deactivation of the 833rd Air Division. However, this time, while Fig got a new leadership title, Mrs. Newton was able to remain in the same home.

Toward the end of 1992, Fig knew what was coming. He and Elouise had never "campaigned" for their next assignment, but it was on the horizon. Fig just did the job to the best of his ability. His three career goals had been first, become a pilot; second, become a Thunderbird pilot; and third, become a wing commander. He had held not just one, not two, but three wing commands. The military system of advancement is based on an approximate two-year rotation. Then it's "called up or out." If the individual is not selected for the next level of promotion, either the person decides to retire or they are directed to do so. The exception is that of colonel. Many officers maintain that rank for longer periods of time.

Lloyd Newton was no longer a colonel. He was now a general officer. Would he be called up? If so, he knew he would definitely be flying a desk the next time around. In evaluating the possibilities, he realized that while he had not held a staff position in quite some time, neither had he ever held a joint job, a position in which he would be working jointly with members of all branches of the services.

Around that time, the Newtons were attending a Commanders' Conference at Tactical Air Command headquarters at Langley Air Force Base, Virginia, when who should walk up but General Mike Loh.

"I know you're wondering," he said, knowing they were anxious about what came next. "They haven't given me the right job yet," Loh said. "When they do, I will call you."

Soon afterward, he called with the news.

Loh began, "I hope you like Tampa, Florida."

"Oh," Fig replied. "Central Command."

"No, the other command," the four-star countered.

General Newton was more than surprised! "What? Special Ops? What do I know about Special Operations?"

"Well," General Loh responded, "they said they want you."

So it was a return to Tampa's MacDill Air Force Base for the Newtons. Goodbye, desert; hello, gulf coast.

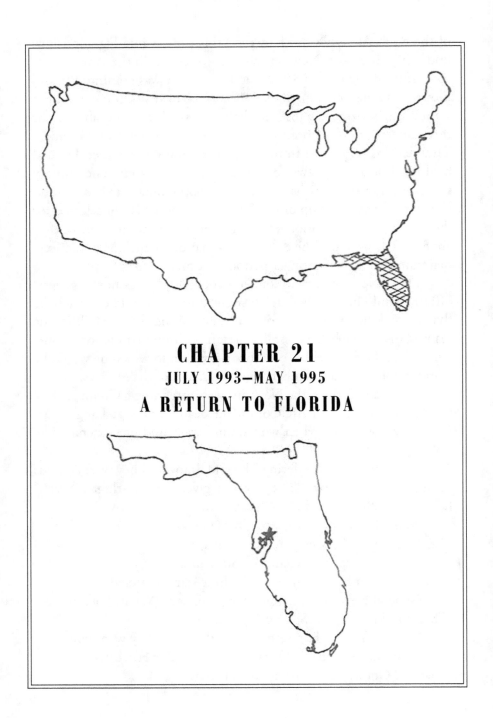

CHAPTER 21
JULY 1993–MAY 1995
A RETURN TO FLORIDA

The General still remembers when General Mike Loh called with the news that he was headed to MacDill. It was "almost like I would have chosen it myself." The couple was happy to be heading to Florida. Fig looked forward to working in a joint-forces environment operating round the clock. His Pentagon years had taught him how effective 24/7 multi-branch collaboration could be. He knew it was vital in the Special Operations arena.

Mrs. Newton would be close to her family in St. Petersburg, just across Tampa Bay. Fig felt his Elouise was due this small reward after all the packing, miles, and places she had been as his Air Force support team (i.e., wife). Living on Bayshore Boulevard in base housing, their new home would be adjacent to the waters of Tampa Bay. That would be nice, too.

Lt. Col. Robert Hooker welcomed the Newtons to MacDill AFB. He would be the General's new Executive Officer. Elouise started her work of organizing another new home as Fig headed to the office. When General Newton reported to the Special Operations Command (SOCOM) Commander, Army General (four-star) Wayne Downing, his first comment was "Sir, I don't know much about Special Operations, but I am happy to be here."

Downing's reply was "Fig, you're just what I want—a different perspective and a different viewpoint of our operations."

Most people there had been in the special operations career field for most of their career. The brass felt that, in addition to Newton's experience, he brought a set of "fresh eyes" to make their unit all the more effective.

Shortly after their arrival, Mrs. Newton helped pin a second star on Fig's shoulders as he was promoted to the rank of Major General. He served as Director of Operations J3 (J for Joint Operations) on the staff of the Commander of US Special Operations Command. The team had American and international representatives. Their daily work held national and global implications about troop deployment, US policies and US engagement around the world.

At any one time, Special Ops had people engaged with allies in over seventy countries. The MacDill AFB team was in constant contact with the Joint Chief of Staff, the Secretary of Defense, and the President. A few of the now de-classified assignments they handled during that time dealt with Somali attacks in Africa and subversive activities by then-relatively-unknown terrorist leader Osama Bin Laden. The General sadly remembered the tragic October 1993 day of an attack in Somalia that became better known as Black Hawk Down, involving the loss of American Special Operation Forces troops in the city of Mogadishu. He would never forget that day.

Fig knew that some of the world's finest soldiers were working together on many independent operations and deployments. Special Ops commanded Delta Force, a multi-services unit of American troops comprised of Air Force Air Commandos, Navy SEALs, and predominately, Army Rangers and Green Berets. Whenever Special Ops Forces' assistance was requested from an international ally, a small unit of operators would deploy to an undisclosed location. The elite team trained abroad, working with and living the same lifestyle as their host countrymen. This commitment built mutual respect and camaraderie among all involved. When the time was right, additional Special Forces members would join other forces, as their talents were required to accomplish the mission.

General Newton remains committed to honoring these brave men. He feels they truly "serve at the pointed end of the spear." Their jobs are as tough as it gets, both physically and mentally. They are proof that a few very bright people can make extraordinary things happen. Only a relative handful of applicants qualify for this duty. The washout rate in selection and training is very high, but better to fail there than in the field.

The Newtons' two years in Tampa were spent in non-stop mode, and the months were speeding by. One Saturday, Fig had returned from his morning jog. He and Elouise were finishing their coffee when the phone rang. It was his old friend, now Chief of Staff of the United States Air Force, General Ron Fogleman, calling from the Pentagon.

She heard Fig saying, "Yes, Sir. No, Sir. Yes, Sir. Yes, Sir. Okay, Sir."

Fig hung up the phone and turned to his wife.

"Well, what was that all about?" she asked. By this time, she was used to strange phone calls at all hours from the SOCOM Commander.

So Fig recounted Fogleman's half of the conversation. "Fig, we want you to come to the Pentagon, and you will be moved up to your third star." He'd just been offered the Assistant Vice-Chief of Staff (A-VICE) job.

"Oh, get out of here. You're kidding me!" exclaimed his wife.

"No. No. Really!" Fig protested. But he had to admit, even he was wondering if it was real. He had been sure MacDill would be his last assignment, that retirement was just around the corner. As Fig sat back down at the table, he saw another exciting assignment and another star. Elouise saw…more packing boxes again!

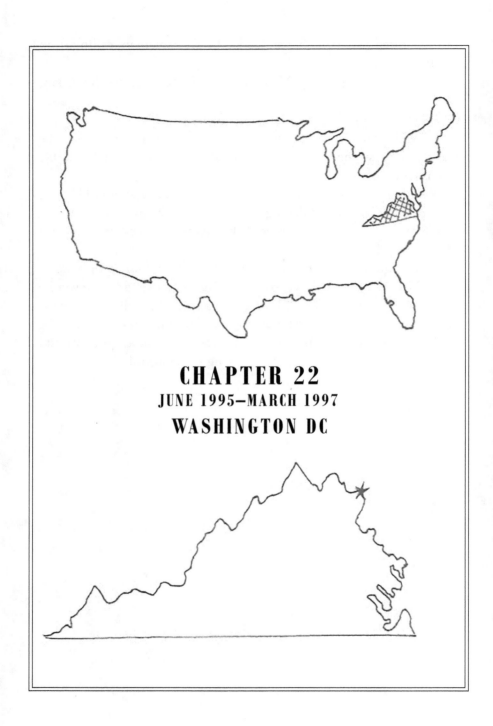

CHAPTER 22
JUNE 1995–MARCH 1997
WASHINGTON DC

The official orders arrived a couple of months later; it was now "Goodbye, Florida," and "Welcome back to DC." During ceremonies held at Boiling AFB, Mrs. Newton helped pin yet another star on her husband's uniform. The new Lieutenant General Lloyd W. "Fig" Newton had come a long way from that January 1965 day when, on his first trip to the nation's capital, he had led his TSU Air Force ROTC Drill Team in President Lyndon Johnson's presidential inaugural parade!

Approximately 250 guests (VIPs, military aids, spouses, etc.) attended the promotion ceremony. In his comments, General Fogleman told the audience, "Fig Newton is from a small town called Ridgeland in South Carolina. I'm sure no one is left there today because (pause) they're all here!" Yes, family, friends, and mentors had all traveled to share in this one glorious moment.

What would be his duties? General Fogleman answered that with a surprise announcement. "I'm sure General Newton thinks he'll have the usual A-VICE experience here at the Pentagon, but two years from now, the Air Force will be celebrating its 50th Anniversary." That's how Fig learned that he was now expected to plan a very special yearlong celebration for the most powerful Air Force of the most powerful nation in the world. And he had barely twenty-four months in which to do it!

Talk about getting busy! He knew from experience that a small, top-notch team was needed at the core of the project. He also knew this task wasn't anything the Chief and Vice Chief of Staff had time to do. It was *his* team's job. They would work closely with others around the globe while helping to direct activities on all Air Force bases. His superiors, however, did have input, such as "I want us to invite every Air Force Commander from every Allied country in the world," said General Fogleman. That meant all ninety-plus of them.

The team developed its theme—"A Golden Legacy and Boundless Future." This would not be just one major event but a yearlong international celebration. Beginning in September of 1996, US air bases abroad and air force bases throughout the United States held individual events. His office gave the outline, theme, logo, and general idea for consistency. Then he expected the local bases to follow through. General Newton was confident that the commanders of each location would do an outstanding job. As an example of the nation-wide cooperation this celebration received, the US Postal Service unveiled a set of commemorative stamps at the Pentagon.[31]

How the excitement spread! For example, Fig received a call from the commander of Wright Patterson AFB near Dayton, Ohio.

"Hey, Fig. I wanna do a marathon run here at Wright Patterson to tie in with the 50th Anniversary. But I want it to be the *first and to live on*." That successful race did become an annual event and continues today as a legacy of that Air Force anniversary.

Nellis AFB, Nevada would host the main event in September 1997. Its Las Vegas location was perfect. The city had the infrastructure, hotel rooms, and facilities needed. A multi-day Commanders Conference (including air shows) was held. International commanders, their spouses and aides were there. From Cambodia to England, the assemblage arrived, resembling a temporary United Nations.

All foreign air attaches serving in the United States were Newton's responsibility. His staff members were the liaisons responsible for each military group as well as international embassy representatives and political leaders. Handling the proper protocol and etiquette for the cultures of over eighty countries was top priority. *Everything*, down to the smallest detail, was coordinated—from arrivals to departures. Plans for transportation, security, terrorist-threat possibilities, mass casualty contingency, and sensitivity to tensions among countries were on the list. Those tensions among guests, though, seemed to dissolve during their stay.

This was the first time in modern history that Russian and United States Air Force commanders had stood together on the same stage. Many other historical firsts occurred during that event.

The air show was viewed by a quarter-of-a-million fans daily. Six demonstrations teams—Japanese, Brazilian, Italian, Jordanian, Canadian, and of course, the USAF Thunderbirds thrilled the crowds.

Individual military and civilian air performers were also part of each show. It was the first time since the end of World War II that the Japanese Air Force had been deployed outside of Japan. The Newton team was responsible for helping the Japanese ship their planes into San Diego and then getting them up to Nevada. All sorts of amazing accomplishments happened!

Everyone on the A-VICE team made the impossible possible. Team Leader, Colonel Mary Tripp, was one of the General's miracle workers. The Pentagon had asked for ideas from throughout the Air Force and beyond. Col. Tripp had the responsibility of reviewing, selecting, and editing the best of these to pass along for implementation. Kid-glove diplomacy and a positive attitude helped her cull through the possibilities.

Another valuable member of the team must also be mentioned here. Mrs. Newton was busy around the clock with hostess responsibilities. International guests and national political dignitaries from around the world were part of her daily schedule. Her protocol and etiquette training came in handy for an occasion such as this. When the Newtons were alone, they would look at each other, smile, and think, *Are we really here?* They felt like pinching themselves for being "lucky" enough to live this American dream.

(Author's note: It should be noted, however, that their "luck" came about through decades of work, sacrifice, and service. They both followed John and Annie's advice of "Just do the best job you can possibly do.")

Early in '97, with the project in full swing, Fig happened to walk down the Pentagon corridor past the Chief of Staff's office.

"Hey, Fig. Come in here a moment," Chief of Staff Fogleman called.

Oh, Fig thought to himself, *he probably wants to 'help me' with another idea to fit into the 50th Anniversary plan.* Fig followed the general into his inner office, then Fogleman closed the door.

"I just want to tell you that the Air Force Secretary and I decided you're going down to replace Billy Boles at Training Command," General Fogleman began. "We sent your name down to the Secretary of Defense for approval."

"I don't know what to say, Sir," was Newton's reply.

"You don't have to say anything. It's already done."

"But, Sir, what about the 50th?" Fig asked.

"Oh, don't worry. You and your team can still take care of that," assured General Fogleman.

What did this conversation mean? Another assignment awaited Fig, and it wouldn't yet be retirement. He would return to Randolph AFB, Texas, to replace retiring General Boles as Commander of Air Education and Training (AE&T) for the entire US Air Force.

Fig knew this meant a *fourth star!* He was totally speechless as he left the Chief's office. Reflecting back, he admits that he had had a pretty good idea over the years, based on the way his career was going, that he might make Brigadier General (one-star), but he *never* had any idea about any of the others!

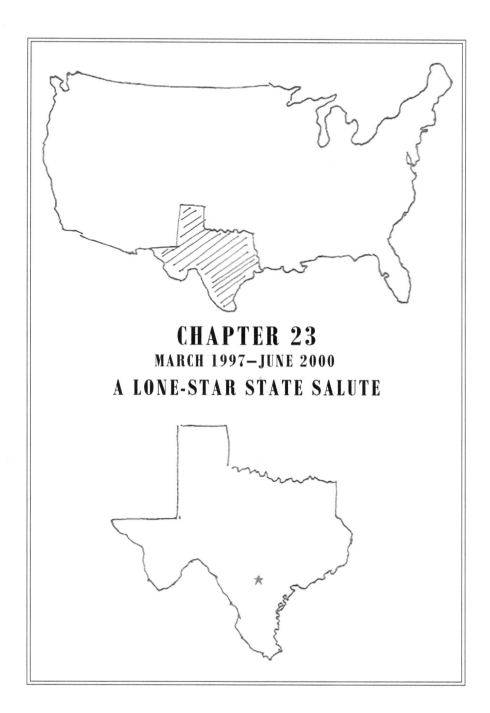

CHAPTER 23
MARCH 1997–JUNE 2000
A LONE-STAR STATE SALUTE

Remembering that all-important four-letter word of his father's, General Newton had to smile when he received his final assignment. He awaited the pinning of his fourth star. He would then become one of only eleven four-star generals in the United States Air Force. (One star, brigadier general; two stars, major general; three stars, lieutenant general; four stars, only one word is needed—*general!*) Four letters from Dad, four stars from the Air Force. They went together rather nicely. K-N-O-W; knowledge; education. This path had opened many doors for the hard-working young man from the Carolina Low Country. His father's wisdom had brought Fig full circle.

In March 1997, the General and Mrs. Newton traveled one more leg of their journey of military service, 1,607 miles, returning to Randolph Air Force Base, Texas. His job was to be Commander, Air Education and Training Command. The assignment, while head-quartered at Randolph, included responsibility for thirteen bases from Panama City, Florida to Spokane, Washington. In addition to 43,000 military personnel, he had 14,000 civilian employees and over 10,000 contractors now under his charge.

Yes, that's right: Fig was to be in charge of all Air Force *education!* He would help spread his father's wisdom to every service man and woman. They could then take their new *know*ledge, discipline, and leadership skills home to *their* children.

The Newtons said another difficult goodbye to Washington and the Pentagon. They had enjoyed a beautiful Maryland home on Andrews Air Force Base and a city filled with long-time friends. They knew that this really would be the last DC goodbye as an active-duty couple. All packed and everything ready for shipping, they pulled out of the Maryland driveway, heading west via South Carolina, always making a visit home whenever possible. Then they turned the car toward their reunion with Texas.

Once at Randolph, they would be moving into the previous home of Gen. Joe Ashy. Fig smiled as he remembered when, on his last Texas tour, "Tough Joe Ashy was beating me up down there." He had realized that the lessons learned from that strong commander had contributed greatly to his future advancement, including the position he would now hold. Leaders train. Future leaders listen and learn.

Elouise and Fig would again be living on one of the most beautiful bases in the United States Air Force. From their home, the couple could turn right and be at the Base Chapel. They could once again walk across the street for a Sunday movie. Yes, this would be another terrific assignment.

The house was ready so they moved right in. A few days later, family and friends arrived. On the first Thursday in March, two ceremonies were held on the same day. The first one included two very important people in the Newton's lives. USAF Chief of Staff, General Fogleman, and his wife, Miss Jane, flew in from DC for the small, private pinning ceremony at the Officers Club. Mrs. Newton stepped forward one last time to pin that fourth star onto her Fig's shoulders. General Lloyd W. "Fig" Newton wore it proudly and deservedly. For the first time in American history, three of the four branches of the armed services had an African-American four-star general serving in its ranks—General Johnny Wilson, US Army; Admiral J. Paul Reason, US Navy; and now, General Lloyd W. "Fig" Newton, US Air Force.

The second ceremony, the Change of Command, was a bit different. Approximately a thousand people—military and community leaders, friends, and family—attended the large affair, filling one of the base hangars. Retired Army Sergeant Major and cousin, Lee Newton, "The Uniform" of Fig's childhood, was there. Ridgeland vacated once again as all of Fig's immediate family, many cousins, and friends were in attendance. Fig and Elouise were happy to have his mom, Annie, Elouise's mom, Ida, and most of their children stay with them in their new home. Fig was especially pleased that his mother was there since his dad was unable to attend. It was hard for her to comprehend all that her little Lloyd had accomplished and experienced since he'd left their small farm in Ridgeland. Her prayers had been answered many times over.

The Change of Command ceremony began. The three generals—Fogleman, Boles, the departing commander, and Newton—marched to the stage. Earlier their wives had been escorted to their seats in the front row. There stood three of the eleven Air Force four-star generals.

Boles passed the organizational flags to Fogleman and Fogleman passed them to Newton. The symbols of the Change of Command were then handed to Newton's senior enlisted advisor, Command Chief Master Sergeant Kenneth Hair. Speeches followed. Gen. Fogleman gave his remarks first. He thanked Gen. Boles for his service to the nation and for his contributions and leadership of Air Education and Training Command. He also welcomed the Newtons to their new assignment.

General Boles, who was retiring, gave his goodbye speech of gratitude, noting the accomplishments by everyone during his tenure. Next, Newton gave a shorter "thank you for the opportunity" speech. General and Mrs. Fogleman had to depart immediately, but their presence had meant a great deal to the Newtons.

After the ceremony, they returned to the Officers' Club for a much larger reception than the one that morning. Many of the town's dignitaries as well as military brass attended. Several of them remembered the Newtons from their previous tour in San Antonio and welcomed them back. The family gathered at the club as well to share in this grand celebration. It was a memorable occasion for everyone.

Later that day, it was business as usual. Arriving at the new office and meeting his staff, Fig was glad to see one familiar face already hard at work. Lt. Col. Fran Hendricks, the only officer to accompany Fig from the Pentagon, was there to help guide the transition of command and to help the staff understand how Fig Newton operated. His staff gave the new four-star the standard orientation and schedule. First, he met with his Vice Commander, Lieutenant General Clark Griffith, a seasoned Training Command veteran who would help Fig better understand the intricate details of the command's training system. Clark's superb knowledge and dedicated support was critical to Fig's success during his early days of command.

The Newtons became fast friends with Clark and his wife Jean, and that friendship continues today.

As commander, Fig would also be working closely with the Command Chief Master Sergeant, Ken Hair, whose job was to help coordinate enlisted personnel issues. The General's schedule showed that he would see the Chief for their first official meeting in three or four days.

Turning to Lt. Col. Hendricks, Newton said, "Why don't you change the schedule and have Chief Hair come to see me this afternoon?" He had two reasons for this request. The way Fig saw it, there were around 5,000 officers in the command, yet Chief Hair cared for approximately 38,000 enlisted personnel. They made up a much larger percentage of the new commander's responsibility. Newton also wanted to send a message to all the Command that the enlisted force was as important to the mission as the officer corps. Just as all pilots and support staff of the Tuskegee Experiment were known as "Tuskegee Airmen," all members of the Air Force, all "*airmen*," were equal in their value to the mission.[32] Looking back, the General reflects, "That was probably one of the *most* important decisions I made while in that command position."

The two leaders developed an extraordinary relationship. "People saw that I wanted to stay very close to my enlisted advisor and the enlisted force." This decision by the new commander was *really huge* to Chief Hair. He truly appreciated the General's show of respect and confidence in him.

Part of Newton's job was recruiting and training. Everyone who enlists in the Air Force, which is about 40,000 people annually, comes through Lackland AFB, in San Antonio, for basic training (also known as boot camp). The Marines report to Parris Island in Beaufort, South Carolina and San Diego, California for training, the Navy recruit training command is at Great Lakes near Chicago. Army recruits then trained only at Ft. Jackson in Columbia, South Carolina. Later, Ft. Benning in Georgia, Ft. Leonard in Wood, Missouri, and Ft. Sill in Oklahoma were added. Additionally, Newton was responsible for all specialty-skill training and all pilot and navigator training that took place in the Air Force.

One day early in his command, Fig suddenly stopped. *What does this assignment mean?* he asked himself. *I am training tomorrow's Air Force. Twenty years from now, it will be impacted by what we're doing now.* He realized the leadership of the twenty-first century was walking around before him. *What kind of brand, training, and culture will develop future leaders?* In this final four-star command, General Newton set a vision and policy of how to train the very best Air Force in the world. He oversaw tens of thousands of hours of training every month. There were over 1,300 airplanes under his command. Just those planes alone would have constituted the sixth largest air force in the world.

Fig always knew that the right people *must* be assigned in the right places to achieve mission success. He would *see* changes in their professional development and in their leadership growth. Having command over thousands of people's lives and careers could be difficult. However, he was totally committed to always being *fair* and *caring*!

From their days at the Armed Forces Staff College, Fig had developed a great working relationship with now Lt. Gen. David McIlvoy. The Newtons had also become great friends with Dave and his wife Leanna. Dave was someone Fig knew he could trust, and he wanted to have the opportunity to work with him again.

When Lieutenant General Clark Griffith announced his retirement, Newton needed a new Vice Commander at Randolph. He petitioned Gen. Fogleman in Washington for permission to move McIlvoy to Texas. Fogleman's answer was "You can't have him now." McIlvoy's current task in the Pentagon was incomplete, and he was still needed on the Air Staff. Fig understood, but he was very glad when, at the right time, Fogelman called, and McIlvoy was on his way to Randolph.

In South Carolina, an aging John Newton's mobility was steadily decreasing. By 1994, Fig and his siblings were concerned about the strain his care was putting on their mom. Don spoke with their father about moving into assisted living. To all his children's surprise, he offered no resistance and agreed to give it a try. Annie spent as much time as possible with her best friend, visiting almost every day. She always brought one of John's favorite snacks, but she would never say anything about it. They would sit, talking for a while, and then John would say, "What do you have in that pocketbook?" Out would come the treats—maybe some orange slices or maybe some other treat. It was one of their private games they played to make life seem a bit more like it used to be. Although he hadn't been able to travel to Randolph for the presentation of Fig's fourth star, Annie brought back pictures and the full story to share with the proud father.

In late 1998, Annie was hospitalized in Beaufort with a blood disorder. Fig and Elouise spent time with her in December before they headed off to Hawaii to celebrate their upcoming tenth anniversary.

John knew she was ill and that was the reason she didn't come by with her daily treats. On January 9, 1999, Fig got a call from the doctor. Annie, 85, had passed away. Fig, Marion, and Don went together to give their father the news. "My Annie! My Annie is gone," John lamented.

The children said that John took her death pretty well. He grieved quietly and privately; that's the way he was. Fig and Elouise stayed in Ridgeland awhile to help him in the transition. But Fig and his siblings knew his father was brokenhearted over the loss of his precious wife of more than seventy years.

Over the next few months, he was doing pretty well. He would talk about the farm and the horses. One spring day, he made a comment: "Annie's not coming back, is she?" In May, Fig got another call, this one, from his brother Marion. Dad, 94, was gone. The nurses had helped him get up that morning and into his favorite chair. He ate his breakfast and went to sleep. It was a peaceful, eternal sleep. After a lifetime together, it was only from January to May that they were apart; only four short months, and they were reunited.

A couple of years later, the General thought of one last lesson that he had learned from his parents' passing. Because John was over eight years older than Annie, he and his siblings had the full expectation that John would die first. Life does not follow "expectations," he was reminded. Enjoy every day.

Command Chief Master Sergeant Hair and the Newtons would sometimes travel together. When they visited air force bases, General and Mrs. Newton would meet with those in leadership, as well as with the troops and their spouses from across the bases. Chief Hair would engage with other enlisted men and women, like the young, single members of the force. He would take a female NCO along to address women's issues, especially with the junior women. But the most important people they all would see on these visits were the young trainees and those doing the training.

Long ago, Fig had decided to stay in the Air Force for one reason: he felt he could have a positive impact on other people's lives. During those base visits, General Newton would ask, "What are the problems you're dealing with that I can help with?" In base-wide meetings, he heard about health care, food service, commissary problems, and other issues that impacted the airmen's daily lives. If armed forces members were unhappy with the treatment of their families, they would be unhappy at work. When people left those meetings, he wanted them to know "the General means what he says. If you want to ask a hard question, here I am. We can't always change it, but we'll try." Many times things were fixed right there on the spot.

One of Fig's key leadership beliefs is you can never have too much information or put too much thought into how to do things. Always seek feedback from others. Always return feedback to others.

Mrs. Newton would meet with air force spouses. As a team player, she knew if you really want to know what's going on, talk to the families. She participated in "Quality Conferences" held at Randolph. Airmen from maintenance through pilots and some spouses would come for full-day symposiums. Spouses played a key role in these seminars, and the leadership had a keen interest in their comments. The next morning, the findings would be formalized into a report, and an action plan would be formed before everyone returned home.

Mrs. Newton continued to represent the Air Force in many ways. She looked after Fig on the home front while she also remained active in the community and on base. They both felt blessed to live such a life and lead others. "You will not pass this way again," she would often remark. She helped them both to be "in the moment" and to relish each opportunity.

Early on June 18, 1999, the general was seated at his desk. His secretary came over and closed his door, which was a bit unusual. Later, she knocked on the door. He walked over and opened it. There, in the outer office, stood Command Chief Master Sergeant Hair and several other chief master sergeants asking permission to see him.

"Sir, may we come in for a moment?" As they were escorted into Newton's office, they closed the door behind them.

Oh, no! shuttered Newton to himself. *What have I done now for all of these chief master sergeants to come see me all at the same time?*

What had he done, indeed? The group of NCOs was there to inform General Lloyd W. "Fig" Newton that he had made "significant contributions to the welfare and prestige of the Air Force enlisted corps' mission effectiveness as well as overall military establishment." For these accomplishments, he was being awarded the prestigious US Air Force Order of the Sword. The enlisted force founded this award, and its members were the only ones who could present it. The recipient would usually be a military senior officer, and it is presented on an irregular basis. No one knows when or who will receive it next.[33]

The Order of the Sword is patterned after two orders of chivalry founded during the Middle Ages in Europe—the Royal Order of the Sword and the Swedish Military Order of the Sword, both of which are still in existence. The noncommissioned officer corps was established early in the twelfth century.

In 1522, King Gustav I of Sweden bid his commissioned noblemen to appoint officers to serve him. The people who became noncommissioned officers would honor their leader and pledge their loyalty by ceremoniously presenting the leader with a sword. It was a symbol of truth, justice, and power rightfully used, serving as a token for all to see and know that here was a leader.

This tradition came to the United States as early as the Revolutionary War and, after years in dormancy, was revived in the 1860's when Gen. Robert E. Lee was presented a sword by his command.[34]

"When they told me, I was so touched, I didn't know how to respond!" Newton still vividly remembers. He and Mrs. Newton were then honored with a dinner and ceremony attended only by enlisted airmen, Chief Master Sergeant Hair, and other NCOs. The Chief Master Sergeant of the Air Force, Eric W. Benken, came from Washington, DC to lead the ceremony. The only officers in attendance were selected by Fig. This honor, humbly accepted by Newton, remains displayed in a prominent place in their home today. Both General and Mrs. Newton placed it there with much gratitude.

Fig's tour at Randolph would normally have lasted two years; however, Chief of Staff Fogleman had retired in 1999. His replacement, Gen. Mike Ryan, had asked Newton to remain for another year for a smoother transition in both of their commands. Fig was delighted and agreed to stay on.

With only a few months left, General Newton began a tour of the thirteen bases in his command to say thanks and goodbye. Their visit to Vance AFB was the hardest and tenderest. They couldn't forget the spontaneous wedding celebration and the support for their son, James, the people of Enid had given them the decade before. On the morning of their departure, the new wing commander, who had only arrived the previous week, came to pick them up. He didn't, though, head over to the flight line and their awaiting plane. Instead, he turned on a parallel street. Fig was thinking that, being new, the commander didn't know exactly where he was going. "Thank goodness this was one time in my life I kept my mouth shut," he later remembered.

As they looked outside the car, they saw that the "wrong street" was totally lined with base personnel and friends from throughout the city who had come to give them a heartfelt and heartwarming sendoff. The Newtons could not put into words how much that meant to them!

In June 2000, a private farewell party was held at a hotel in San Antonio. Military and civilian guests from around the country gathered to honor the Newtons. Two old friends surprised them. Senior Master Sergeant Danny Showers was there. They had served together when Fig was a Congressional Liaison. Chief Master Sergeant Walt

Richardson had worked with the new captain in the Philippines and kept in touch with Fig throughout his career. Fig always said Chief "grew me all the way from a new young captain up to a four-star general."

With three days left, the General took to the air in a T-38 for his last official active-duty flight. After the standard briefing, he lifted off for a training mission, a couple of touch-and-gos, and a fly-by. In the landing pattern, he called to the tower, "Spur-01 Final Landing." (He had taken his Randolph call sign from the San Antonio Spurs.) When he taxied in, Air Force fire trucks were waiting, spraying arches of water over his T-38 in a final tribute. Elouise was there, too, to join in a champagne farewell toast with those on duty.

A few days prior to "R-Day" (retirement), the Newtons had moved from their base home into the Distinguished Visitors' Quarters. The day of the Change of Command, the Newtons' good friends, Chief of Staff Gen. Mike Ryan and his wife, Jane, flew down from Washington, DC. The ceremony commenced, with Fig's role now reversed. After the speeches, Fig and Elouise said their good-byes. A long line of cars filed slowly toward the Officers' Club. The Newtons' car made a different turn. They would not attend the reception in honor of the new commander. Their job was finished. This protocol is important for military discipline and loyalty. The American public most often watches this tradition during the changes of the nation's commanders-in-chief. Outgoing US presidents do not attend the inaugural balls and receptions of the incoming president. This strengthens the institutions of leadership.

The Newtons' official car, complete with the four-star general's flags attached, returned them to the Distinguished Visitors' Quarters one last time. Back in their suite, they changed into traveling clothes. As 57-year-old Lloyd W. "Fig" Newton took off the uniform he had respected since childhood and had worn for thirty-four years of service, he paused and then thought, *Well, I certainly won't have this on for any active duty…anymore.*

In thirty minutes, they and their suitcases were in their own car, private citizens once again. Driving through that Randolph Air Force

Base gate for the *last time* is a bittersweet memory General Lloyd W "Fig" Newton will never forget.

They headed east toward home. While stopping over in one of their favorite cities, New Orleans, for a few days, Elouise turned to Fig. "You've really gotten us in a fix this time. We're jobless and homeless all at the same time!" she teased. Her sense of humor was as invaluable as ever.

Dottie greeted them as they pulled into the Newton family farm. When she had retired from the Northeast, she returned home and built a house just down the road from her parents. With their deaths the previous year, she moved back to The Farm to help keep it up. Elouise and Fig stayed with her for two-and-a-half months, from June through September. Fig spent a lot of time on his dad's tractor, letting the close of his thirty-four-plus years of service settle around him.

Small Jasper County/Ridgeland, South Carolina is home to two Air Force four-star generals—one black, Lloyd W. "Fig" Newton, and one white, Jacob E. Smart. They both went away to serve and continued to return home to honor their roots. The generals met and became friends in the early '90s. The Newtons often visited with him when they came home to Ridgeland. General Smart passed away in 2006 at the age of ninety-seven. Today Fig is fondly referred to as one of "Ridgeland's Favorite Sons." He reached that status by learning from the family and friends who nurtured him in that Carolina homeland—"Always do your best," "Be true to yourself," and most importantly, "Do unto others as you would have them do unto you." That Golden Rule planted deep in his Low Country character, led to a lifetime of *true* riches—friends, family, opportunities for new experiences in leadership, and joy of service.

How tall is a Giant? This one is 5 feet 10 1/2 inches. That's big enough to touch the sky, circle the globe, improve thousands of lives, and give his country "the very best he could."

"I would do it all over again!"

—LW "F" N

EPILOGUE

2000–PRESENT

The Newtons may have been temporarily "homeless," but Fig was "jobless" for only two-and-a-half months. (At least he was without a good job offer only that long.) After leaving San Antonio on their way back to Ridgeland, they stopped to visit a good friend and wing command at Tyndall AFB near Panama City, Florida. The General was on the golf course when his new civilian cellphone rang. It was a call from Pratt & Whitney, an aircraft engines manufacturing company.

"I want to talk to you about a job," the conversation began.

"I just got rid of one of those," Fig replied jokingly.

Strict, no-conflict-of-interest regulations demand that retiring military personnel should not be approached about future civilian employment until *after* they have fully separated from the service. Fig had sent out no resumes or "feelers." He was adamant that he would have no divided loyalties at any time in his military career. He needed time to relax with his family and to consider exactly what his next step would be.

"I could not work for a company whose core values didn't align with my own. [The job] was not only about money but also job satisfaction."

There are myriad corporations around the world servicing and supplying the US military. Fig knew involvement in this field would be an exciting way to transition to the next season of his life. But he would take his time and choose carefully. In September 2000, he did begin work with Pratt & Whitney in Hartford, Connecticut, a company that designs, develops, and manufactures aircraft engines. The retired general's expertise was a perfect match for this US-based aerospace company with worldwide operations. For five and a half years, Fig and Elouise enjoyed New England, a region of America in which, despite all their moves, they had *not* lived before.

This transitional employment gave them time to plan their retirement. Where had the couple been happiest? Where could they be close to family? Where would their five children like to come for a visit or perhaps live nearby? Their Florida assignment at MacDill had been great. The Texas hill country was beautiful. Arizona had wonderful year-round weather. They had lived in some pretty nice places!

Finally the choice was made. Beginning in November 2005, the Tampa Bay area became their new home. It was a timely move in many ways. Elouise still had family in the area, and they had several retired friends there.

Their son, Bernard, lived in Tampa with two of their grandchildren. James had taken a new job in Gainesville at the Veterans' Administration (VA) Hospital, only a couple of hours north on I-75. The family really enjoyed getting together whenever possible.

Tampa turned out to be just the right spot for the Newtons. They had made many great memories there when Fig was in the service, and they were now happily making more. Speaking of memories, Fig still laughs when he recalls this story:

One sunny Florida day, the couple was driving over to Pinellas County to see family. Fig was in a feisty fighter-pilot-general mood. Just in case his wife might forget, he was teasingly reminding her of how lucky she was to be married to him. "There aren't that many four-star generals out there," he continued with a sly grin. "Why, just look at that fellow over there," he said, calling attention to a man going to work at a different job. "You're lucky you married me. You might have married him and then how different your life would have been."

Ellie, riding along beside him, quietly took in his humor. Pausing to observe the worker to whom Fig was referring and then returning the glint in Fig's eyes with one of her own, she replied, "No, Sweetheart, *your* life would have been different. If I had married that man, *he* would have been the four-star general, just like you!"

Service was in General Newton's blood. Retirement wasn't going to change that. Because of his lifelong commitment to education, he has continued working with scouting, school systems, Girls and Boys Clubs, and other organizations around the country.

When speaking with young people, he is very honest about setting and reaching goals. "What's important for them is to continue to develop themselves to reach the summit they're trying to reach. The opportunities are out there. That doesn't mean it's going to be easy. It doesn't mean that someone won't try to stand in his or her way. They have to learn how to negotiate themselves around those problems. Education is the key. It helps to level the playing field."

Newton is actively involved in several military alumni organizations associated with his different commands. He also serves on corporate boards of directors and is involved in his community. The Newtons are still very much on the go.

In 2006, General Newton joined approximately one thousand military-affiliated people to honor the 25th Anniversary of the F-117 Stealth Fighter and the contributions it made to this nation's defense. In his address to the audience Fig noted, "The F-117s…have done great things for our nation. Whenever its nation called, the F-117 answered." *This exact statement can be said of Lloyd Newton and the men and women with whom he served.*

When asked about his next goal, General Newton replied, "I just want to give back."

APPENDICES

APPENDIX 1

LESSONS IN LEADERSHIP

Newton had absorbed natural leadership lessons from his parents and other mentors of his youth in both South Carolina and Tennessee. Throughout his career, he learned through training and observation to identify those characteristics necessary to develop his own leadership style. As he rose in the ranks, it was also necessary for him to recognize traits in others that would lead to the success of the mission at hand. What did he look for?

*****

When he was a boy, a USAF Master Sergeant had impacted Fran Hendricks's life just as Fig's own Army-Sergeant-Major cousin had influenced his. Hendricks, from Pennsylvania, had been adopted and raised by one.

Hendricks and Newton had met prior to working together when then-Lt. Hendricks was an aide to a two-star general in Korea. They hooked up again in Tampa at MacDill's Special Operations Command. Fig wanted Fran to accompany him to his next Washington DC assignment, but he knew that Fran's wife, Connie, had a good job in Tampa. She answered his question about a possible move with an enthusiastic "Oh, yes, I'll go to Washington!" The Hendricks family was committed to the military with their "go where the job needs doing" attitude. The two couples were later stationed together in San Antonio and have enjoyed many years of friendship.

General Newton could count on Hendricks to connect with and encourage people to work together. He just had the knack for making things happen the right way. Following the Texas years, Hendricks went back into military human resources. In June 2012, he, too, became a general officer with his first star. Contemplating retirement, he accepted the presidency of his alma mater, Pennsylvania College, where he would continue using those skills first instilled by his adoptive parents. His family was also looking forward to the graduation of their son from Yale.

*****

Keeping in touch with people one has met along life's journey is a *very* important professional and social skill for anyone to develop and practice. It demonstrates caring and respect for the impact others have made on one's life. More importantly, it builds friendships and memories that make life much richer! Fig Newton was a natural at this, always willing to dedicate the energy necessary to keep connections alive.

Tom Smoot had been part of the 18th Fighter Wing in Okinawa when Fig was Air Force Assistant Vice Chief of Staff. They had met at Randolph AFB, Texas, in 1990 and again while the Newtons were traveling to Singapore. A few months after this meeting, Tom was again transferred to Randolph. When Fran Hendricks transitioned back to his specialty field of personnel/human resources, Fig asked Tom to join his staff as his Executive Officer. Fig remembers Tom's humble and honest approach to life. "I'm just an 'ol country boy, and I don't always know too much." Well, when Tom began either a conversation or an assignment like this comment, watch out! The man was brilliant, dedicated, and most capable! His ability to put others at ease was one of his best assets for getting things done. He and his wife Tammy were also good friends with Elouise and Fig. As Fig's Executive Officer, Tom made sure to take good care of both Fig *and* Elouise whenever they traveled.

Completing the puzzle of positive team building is necessary for both short-term jobs and long-range goals. Fig wasn't sure of the long-range implications, but he knew he had a solution to a short-term need when he requested that Tom Smoot be assigned to him following Hendricks' San Antonio departure.

Smoot, like Hendricks, went on to the rank of General. In fact, Fran Hendricks and Tom Smoot were both on the same list for one-stars. One wonders just how much Fig Newton had to do with that! (Another leadership trait picked up from General Joe Ashy.) Smoot's last assignment was Commandant of the Joint Forces College, Norfolk, Virginia. Following retirement and the loss of his father, he moved back to his home near Knoxville, Tennessee to be close to his mother. Leaders take care of their own too. In retirement, Fig and Tom are still in touch with each other. Tom landed a job with an aerospace company in Knoxville. They often cross paths at aviation conventions and reconnect.

*****

When Lt. Colonel Smoot came to work for Fig, the General was also in need of a new aide-de-camp. The previous aide had flown with Fig in the past and had returned to the cockpit fulltime. As one pilot to another, Fig could certainly understand that. Yet as he culled over the folder of resumes looking for a replacement, Fig was well aware of both the opportunity and the responsibility he was about to ask of some young officer. Narrowing the list to three or four, he was discussing it with Smoot. (Discussing decisions, while seeking and respecting the opinions of other team members, builds a stronger team and a stronger working relationship.)

First impressions, political attitudes, stated and unstated prejudices, and political correctness—these are some of the snags that can make a decision more difficult than it should be. This situation arose when Tom offered, "I've got one more for you, Sir." General Newton hesitated a bit when he saw the resume Tom handed him. Here again, Smoot's "I'm just an 'ol country boy (but I'm gonna get the job done)" persona came out.

"Now, Sir, I know what you're thinking," Smoot offered.

"What am I thinking?" Newton replied.

"I didn't give you this resume because he is African-American. I gave it to you because he is really good!" The resume Smoot gave the general was that of a black Air Force captain.

After interviewing Smoot's candidate, General Newton had a tough decision ahead. As Trent Edwards sat across from him, Fig asked, "Suppose you don't get this job. What will you do with your career?"

"Well, Sir, I'll go back to my job and do the very best I can," replied Edwards.

"Okay, you're hired," said Newton.

It took a couple of seconds for Fig's response to sink in with the young officer across the desk. Then Trent Edwards got up and began doing for the General what he had always done in the past—the very best he could. Tom Smoot, "good 'ol boy," had made another great call.

As Aide-de-Camp, Edwards organized the schedule, arranged for and traveled with the Newtons, and spent a lot of time with the family during the course of a professional day. It is always a tough decision when choosing a replacement because the aide not only has a difficult job but also often becomes like a member of the family. Trent did all of the above while just doing his job "the very best" he could.

Edwards soon had Elouise Newton totally in his court. She truly respected and counted on this young man, remarking at one time, "My, goodness, he'll make a general officer one day." Trent remained with the Newtons until Fig's retirement. He made Colonel a few years ago. In June 2012, when he took over as Commander of a Wing in Montgomery, Alabama, Elouise was present. She represented the retired General, who was unavailable, at Edwards's Change of Command ceremony. Yes, she was there, just like a member of the family would be. (A few years later, Trent Edwards was promoted to Brigadier General, just like Fran Hendricks and Tom Smoot.)

*****

During the demanding preparations for the USAF's 50th Anniversary, all members of Fig's handpicked team were concentrating on making the impossible possible. Colonel Mary Tripp proved invaluable. The task force had solicited ideas and suggestions from throughout the US Air Force, from civilian and political leaders, and from other parties both in and outside of the military. Colonel Tripp was given the responsibility of selecting the best of these for implementation. In the process, she had to handle the pressure of those maybe-not-so-good ideas from important contributors. How does one pass over the suggestions of a congressman or a mayor or a general who was absolutely certain their idea would be just the thing for success?

Somehow from out of the wing-high stacks of entries, she managed to pare down the possibilities to the best of the best. She simultaneously tempered the feelings of those whose requests were passed over, making everyone feel appreciated and valued. While she maintained the high standards necessary for the event, she also made the tough calls to get the job done. All this she accomplished with graceful tact.

*****

North Carolina native, Steven Steele, like Lloyd Newton back in Jasper County, had decided on a military career when he was just a boy. He was a member of his high school's Junior ROTC program. Steele, as everyone called him, was stationed at Randolph Air Force Base, San Antonio, Texas, right after his initial skill training. The young Airman suddenly found himself going from driver's training classes to actually driving senior officers as a transportation specialist.

When Mrs. Newton met the General's new personal driver, she immediately wanted to adopt him, thinking how young an airman he was. Young, it was true, but levelheaded too. He took his assignment most seriously. A passion for promptness and his respectful attitude showed that "doing a job to the best of your ability" had been taught across the state line in North Carolina too.

On one of his trips north to the Pentagon, Fig asked his new aide, Captain Edwards, to make arrangements for Steele to travel with them. Fig was planning to surprise his young driver. Their route would unexpectedly detour to his Mt. Gilead, North Carolina hometown, where they would visit Steele's high school and the local Air Force recruiter. When the car pulled up to the school, who should walk out of the door but Steele's grandfather! The two spent a half-day together with the school's principal while mentoring the current Junior ROTC members. Steele was passing forward his new knowledge, aware that sharing these experiences would encourage those who, only slightly younger than he, had chosen the same path of service. The sooner the lesson learned: the sooner the benefits realized.

Steven left the military at the end of his first tour. Deciding San Antonio was a great place to settle, he now works for the Randolph Air Force Base transportation section as a civilian. He remains part of the extended Newton family, especially close with Mrs. Newton. The phone will ring in Florida, and Elouise will hear: "Hi. Mrs. Newton, Happy Mother's Day." On another day, Fig will hear, "Hi, Sir. This is Steele. Just wanted to check in." Indeed, the energy and discipline expended to keep in touch with others is always worth the effort.

*****

Dave McIlvoy and his wife, Leanna, had known Fig Newton since 1978 when the two then-majors had attended the Armed Forces Staff College together in Norfolk, Virginia. McIlvoy was serving in the Pentagon when Fig requested him as his Vice Commander of Air Education and Training Command at Randolph AFB. This would mean a third star. When the McIlvoys arrived at Randolph, Leanna's and Elouise's casual acquaintance blossomed into a deep friendship. Choosing McIlvoy was part of General Newton's goal of having *full* team players on his staff. He planned to give them the responsibility and the opportunity to make autonomous decisions. "If I'm not available," he let it be known, "the Vice Commander *will* make decisions without me." Fig totally trusted Dave and his abilities. Dave had full authority to make decisions while Fig was away.

*****

There are important leaders in the military that don't necessarily salute. General Newton's admiration for all military spouses, children, and extended families is unbounded. Keeping the "home fires burning" while the airmen are away comes with a very short job description—they do it all, all by themselves, 24/7/365. They do the home management, homework supervision, hold down the second jobs, handle the finances, and the sicknesses and the sports practices and the music lessons and the dance recitals and…well, everything. When it comes time to move, they pack up and say their goodbyes. Then they unpack, organize, and start anew.[35]

Legacy
By Debby Giusti

I am an Air Force wife—a member of that sisterhood of women who have had the courage to watch their men fly off into battle and the strength to survive until their return. Our sorority knows no rank, for we earn our membership with a marriage license, traveling over miles or over nations to begin a new life with our husbands.

Within days, we turn a barren, echoing building into a home, and though our quarters are inevitably white walled and un-papered, we decorate with the treasures of our travels for we shop the markets of the globe.

Using hammer and nail, we tack our pictures to the wall and our roots to the floor as firmly as if we had lived there for a lifetime. We hold a family together by the bootstraps and raise the best of brats, instilling in them the motto, "Home is Togetherness," whether motel or guesthouse, apartment or duplex.

As Air Force wives, we soon realize that the only good in "Goodbye" is the "Hello again." For as salesmen for freedom, our husbands travel far from home, leaving us behind for a week, a month, an assignment. During the separation, we guard the home front, existing till the homecoming.

Unlike our civilian counterparts, we measure time not by age but by tours—married at Lackland, a baby born at Travis, a promotion in England. We plant trees and never see them grow tall, work on projects completed long after our departure, and enhance our community for the betterment of those who come after us. We leave a part of ourselves at every stop.

Through experience, we have learned to pack a suitcase, a car, or hold baggage and live indefinitely from the contents within, and though our fingers are sore from the patches we have sewn and the silver we have shined, our hands are always ready to help those around us.

Women of peace, we pray for a world in harmony, knowing that the flag for which our husbands fight will also blanket them in death. Yet we are an optimistic group, thinking of the good and forgetting the bad, cherishing yesterday while anticipating tomorrow.

Never rich by monetary standards, our hearts are overflowing with a wealth of experiences common only to those united by the special tradition of military life. We pass on the legacy to every Air Force bride, welcoming her with outstretched arms, with love and friendship, from one sister to another, sharing in the bounty of our unique, fulfilling Air Force way of life.

(Author's note: while the above poem is gender-and-relationship specific, it embodies the commitment of every military couple and family, all of you who are "united by the special tradition of military life." I offer my sincere thanks to each and every one of you.—B.J. Harvey Hill)

APPENDIX 2

A JOURNEY OF MILES[36]

The chart below shows the distances General Newton traveled from one tour of duty to the next. Any on-the-job miles have not been compiled. There is no record for the distances on military sorties, training flights, travel on diplomatic missions, inter-base travel throughout the United States, Thunderbird appearances, and other Air Force travel. Recorded in his stacks of logbooks are thousands of flight hours/miles not listed. He definitely qualifies as more than a million-miler.

General Fig Newton Military Travels*

	Origination	APT ID	Destination	APT ID	Statute	Nautical
					Miles	Miles
1	Ridgeland, SC	3J1	Nashville, TN	BNA	410	357
2	Boston, MA	BOS	Williams AFB, Chandler, AZ	IWA	2286	1986
3	Willams AFB, Chandler, AZ	IWA	Davis Monthan AFB, Tuscon, AZ	DMA	91	79
4	Davis Monthan AFB, Tuscon, AZ	DMA	George AFB, Victorville, CA	VCV	411	357
5	George AFB, Victorville, CA	VCV	Ridgeland, SC	3J1	2094	1819
6	Ridgeland, SC	3J1	Spokane, WA	GEG	2174	1888
7	Spokane, WA	GEG	San Francisco, CA	SFO	733	637
8	San Francisco, CA	SFO	Clark AB, Philippines	CRK	6978	6062
9	Clark AB, Philippines	CRK	Da Nang AB, Vietnam	DAD	826	717
10	Da Nang AB, Vietnam	DAD	Norton AFB, San Bernardino, CA	SBD	7875	6841
11	Norton AFB, San Bernardino, CA	SBD	Los Angeles, CA	LAX	68	59
12	Los Angeles, CA	LAX	Savannah, GA	SAV	2152	1869
13	Ridgeland, SC	3J1	George AFB, Victorville, CA	VCV	2094	1819
14	George AFB, Victorville, CA	VCV	Clark AB, Philippines	CRK	7325	6363
15	Clark AB, Philippines	CRK	Luke AFB, Phoenix, AZ	LUF	7604	6606
16	Luke AFB, Phoenix, AZ	LUF	Nellis AFB, Las Vegas, NV	LSV	239	208
17	Nellis AFB, Las Vegas, NV	LAS	Norfolk, VA	ORF	2140	1859
18	Norfolk, VA	ORF	Nellis AFB, Las Vegas, NV	LSV	2140	1859
19	Nellis AFB, Las Vegas, NV	LSV	Pentagon, Washington, DC	DCA	2078	1806
20	Pentagon, Washington, DC	DCA	Beijing, China	PEK	6933	6023
21	Beijing, China	PEK	Pentagon, Washington, DC	DCA	6933	6023
22	Pentagon, Washington, DC	DCA	Capetown, South Africa	CPT	7904	6866
23	Capetown, South Africa	CPT	Pentagon, Washington, DC	DCA	7904	6866
24	Pentagon, Washington, DC	DCA	MacDill AFB, Tampa, FL	MCF	822	714
25	MacDill AFB, Tampa, FL	MCF	Seoul, South Korea	ICN	7564	6576
26	Seoul, South Korea	ICN	Ogden, UT	OGD	5884	5112
27	Ogden, UT	OGD	Washington, DC	DCA	1850	1607
28	Washington, DC	DCA	Vance AFB, Enid, OK	WDG	1149	998
29	Vance AFB, Enid, OK	WDG	Randolph AFB, San Antonio,TX	SAT	474	411
30	Randolph AFB, San Antonio, TX	SAT	Holloman AFB, Alamagordo, NM	ALM	500	435
31	Holloman AFB, Alamagordo, NM	ALM	MacDill AFB, Tampa, FL	MCF	1251	1440
32	MacDill AFB, Tampa, FL	MCF	Pentagon, Washington, DC	DCA	822	714
33	Pentagon, Washington, DC	DCA	Randolph AFB, San Antonio, TX	SAT	1381	1199
	Total flights (assignments only)				**101089**	**88175**

* **Flights do not include air combat or Thunderbird exhibition schedule.** All travel assumed from known USAF base

or closest commercial airfield. Mileage estimates from Flight Manager, Collings Aerospace (formerly Rockwell Collins).

APPENDIX 3

AIRCRAFT AND AWARDS[37]

Aircraft

General Lloyd "Fig" Newton is rated as a Command Pilot. He has logged over 4,000 flight hours in seven military aircraft (T = Trainer; F = Fighter; C = Cargo).

T-37
T-38
F-4
F-15
F-16
F-117
C-12

Military Awards and Decorations

Rank: Commissioned 1966: Second Lieutenant
Retired 2000: General (four-star)
Individual Awards:
Defense Distinguished Service Medal
Air Force Distinguished Service Medal with oak leaf cluster
Legion of Merit with oak leaf cluster
Distinguished Flying Cross with oak leaf cluster
Meritorious Service Medal with oak leaf cluster

Air Medal with sixteen oak leaf clusters
Air Force Commendation Medal
Air Force Outstanding Unit Award with "V" device and two oak leaf clusters
Vietnam Service Medal
Philippine Presidential Unit Citation
Republic of Vietnam Campaign Medal

Civilian Awards for Military Service

1997 Honorary Doctorate in Aeronautical Science,
Embry-Riddle Aeronautical University
Daytona Beach, Florida

1998 Induction into The South Carolina Aviation Hall of Fame
Owens Field
Columbia, South Carolina

1999 Honorary Doctor of Science Degree
Benedict College
Columbia, South Carolina

2012 Ridgeland, South Carolina
I-95 Exit 21 is named in honor of Gen. Lloyd W. "Fig" Newton by the Ridgeland Town Council and Mayor

APPENDIX 4

The importance of respect learned through the Air Force Equal Opportunity and Treatment programs changed the lives of countless service personnel and, in turn through their examples, the lives of countless Americans. The following fable, by an anonymous author, carries much the same message: respect through communication.

> There once was a little boy who had a bad temper. His father gave him a bag of nails and told him that every time he lost his temper he would have to hammer a nail into the back yard fence.
>
> The first day, the boy had to drive 27 nails into the fence.
>
> Over the next few weeks, as he learned to control his anger, the number of nails hammered daily gradually dwindled. He discovered it was easier to hold his temper than to drive those nails into the hard wood. Finally the day came when the boy didn't lose his temper at all. He told his father about it and the father suggested that the boy now pulls out one nail each day that he was able to hold his temper.
>
> The days passed and the young boy was finally able to tell his father that all the nails were gone. The father took his son by the hand and led him to the fence.

"You have done well, my son," the father said, "but look at the holes in the fence. The fence will never be the same.

When you say things in anger, your words leave scars just like those you see here. It won't matter how many times you say 'I'm sorry,' for the wound will still be there."

—Anonymous

APPENDIX 5

March 24, 1999

W hile in his final tour at Randolph AFB, General Newton presented this article at the Eaker Institute Colloquies. It was later published in the newsletter, *Air Force Association*.

> We do not choose our conflicts; instead, they choose us. We must be prepared to fight on any battlefield with any enemy and those enemies have learned that while they might not be able to defeat us outright on the battlefield, there are many other places where they can find vulnerabilities and take advantage of those.
>
> One of those vulnerabilities will certainly be in the minds of the American people or its leadership or its military. We all know that the ultimate center of gravity is the hearts and minds of the people.[38]

These words presented a chilling foreshadowing of the events of September 11, 2001.

APPENDIX 6

HEADLINES OF 1942–2000

T op news stories from *(each noted year)* (source: infoplease.com, June 16, 2014):

1942

After the Japanese attack at Pearl Harbor, 120,000 Japanese and Japanese American citizens were forced to move to "relocation centers" throughout the United States for the remainder of the World War II

1943

The Internal Revenue Service begins withholding taxes on wages

1944

Allied Forces invade Normandy, France on D-Day (June 6)

1945

Germany surrenders May 7 after Hitler suicide. V-E (Victory in Europe) Day (May 8)

America drops atomic bombs on two Japanese cites; Japan surrenders on V-J (Victory in Japan) Day (September 2)

1946

First automatic electronic digital computer ENIAC, University of Pennsylvania

1947

Jackie Robinson joins the Brooklyn Dodgers (#42); first African American in the major leagues

1948

President Harry S. Truman ends racial segregation in the US military

1949

Communist People's Republic of China proclaimed by Chairman Mao Zedong

1950

Charles Schultz introduces the *Peanuts* comic strip

1951

D.J. Alan Freed uses the term *Rock 'n Roll* to introduce rhythm and blues to a broader white audience

1952

King George VI of England dies, his daughter ascends to throne as Queen Elizabeth II

1953

Edmund Hillary of New Zealand and Tensing Norgay of Nepal make the first summit of Mt. Everest

1954

In the court case *Brown v. Board of Education of Topeka*, the US Supreme Court unanimously bans racial segregation in public schools *(but it would take years for it to be implemented throughout the country)*

1955

Albert Einstein dies

1956

Elvis Presley has several hit records and becomes "King of Rock 'n Roll"

1957

The Space Age begins when Russia launches Sputnik I, the first earth-orbiting satellite

1958

NASA begins Project Mercury. Its goal: launch a man into space in two years

1959

Alaska and Hawaii become the 49th and 50th states

1960

John F. Kennedy defeats Richard M. Nixon for president; seventy million people watch the first televised presidential debate

First working laser is built: T. H. Maiman (US)

1961

Soviet Major Yuri A. Gagarin becomes first man in space

Navy Commander Alan B. Shepard Jr. becomes the first US astronaut in space

1962

Unimation introduces the first industrial robot

1963

The civil rights "March on Washington" rally is held by 200,000 blacks and whites on the Mall in Washington, DC; Dr. Martin Luther King Jr. makes his famous "I Have a Dream" speech

President John F. Kennedy is shot and killed in Dallas, Texas

1964

The Beatles perform in the United States on the Ed Sullivan Show

The Grateful Dead and Bob Dylan become popular counter-culture and social-activist musical artists

1965

The first US combat troops arrive in Vietnam; 190,000 soldiers present by the end of the year

1966

The first *Star Trek* episode, "The Man Trap" is broadcast

1967

Thurgood Marshall sworn in as first black US Supreme Court justice
Dr. Christiaan N. Barnard and team of South African surgeons perform world's first successful human heart transplant

1968

Dr. Martin Luther King Jr. is assassinated in Memphis, Tennessee

1969

Apollo 11 astronauts Neil A. Armstrong and Edwin E. "Buzz" Aldrin Jr. first to walk on moon
Children's Television Workshop introduces *Sesame Street*

1970

Bar codes (computer-scanned binary signal code) are introduced in England

1971

US Supreme Court rules unanimously that busing of students may be done to achieve racial desegregation

1972

Electronic mail (e-mail) is introduced

President Nixon makes visit to Communist China and meets with Chairman Mao Tse-Tong (Zedong)

1973

US Secretary of State Henry Kissinger and Le Duc Tho of North Vietnam share the Nobel Peace Prize

1974

Richard Nixon resigns as President of the United States due to the Watergate political scandal

1975

Saigon, Vietnam is surrendered and the remaining Americans are evacuated; the Vietnam War ends

1976

The United States of America celebrated its Bicentennial on July 4th

1977

The movie *Star Wars* premieres

1978

Sony introduces the first portable stereo, the Walkman

1979

Iranian militants capture the US embassy in Teheran and take hostages

1980

Ted Turner broadcasts CNN, the first all-news network

1981

President Ronald Reagan nominates Sandra Day O'Connor as the first woman on US Supreme Court
IBM introduces the first personal computer running Microsoft software

1982

Michael Jackson releases *Thriller*; it becomes biggest-selling album in history

1983

Compact discs (CDs) are introduced

1984

Apple introduces Macintosh personal computer

1985

Three different terrorist groups captured a TWA airliner, an Italian cruise ship and a Boeing 737 airliner

1986

Philippine President Ferdinand Marcos leaves the country after ruling for twenty years
Space shuttle *Challenger* explodes right after launch at Cape Canaveral, Florida

1987

International environmental treaty calls for 50% reduction in use of CFCs (carbon fluorocarbons) to protect the ozone layer in the atmosphere

1988

NASA scientist, James Hansen warns of the dangers of global warming and the greenhouse effect

1989

First World Wide Web server and browser developed by Tim Berners-Lee (England)

1990

South Africa frees Nelson Mandela after twenty seven and a half years in prison

1991

Persian Gulf War (January 16–April 6)

1992

US military leaves Philippines after a hundred years

1993

South Africa throws off apartheid and adopts majority rule

1994

Major League Baseball players go on strike; there is no World Series

1995

Rock and Roll Museum opens in Cleveland, Ohio in a building designed by renowned architect I.M. Pei

1996

Scientists clone the first sheep

1997

Princess Diana of Great Britain is killed in an automobile accident
Harry Potter and the Philosopher's Stone (British title) by J. K. Rolling is published in United Kingdom

1998

The *euro* is established as the single currency throughout most of Europe

1999

The number of Internet users worldwide reaches 150 million

2000

Four-star USAF General Lloyd W. "Fig" Newton retires

NOTES

Preface

1. Sawyer Ashton, Patricia, and Ray E. Ashton Jr., *The Gopher Tortoise, A Life History*, (Sarasota, FL: Pineapple Press, Inc., 2004. Print). Accessed March 16, 2020, en.m.wikipedia.org.
2. "The Town of Ridgeland, South Carolina," Accessed March 26, 2011, www.ridgelandsc.gov.
3. Kelly Champlin, "Veteran Cope Takes Flight," *Jasper County Sun,* November 9, 2011: 1, 5. Print.

Chapter 1

4. "Fighting the U-Boats; US Navy Tenth Fleet Fights the U-Boats," Accessed February 24, 2014, www.uboat.net/allies/ships/us_10thfleet/htm.
5. Reedy, Jr., James R., "Coast Guard Sinking of U-352," Accessed February 24, 2014, http://diodon349.com/war/CG%20sinks%20U352.htm.
6. "Preserve History 1942-A Time of Attack," Accessed February 24, 2014, http://sunkenshipsobx.com/ships_1942.html.
7. The primary sources for the information in this work are personal interviews, telephone interviews, and electronic correspondence with General Lloyd Newton from July 2011 through May 2020. Statements in quotes throughout the text without specific notation are those from General Newton during said interviews.

8. "Plantation," Accessed August 16, 2012, en.m.wikipedia.org.
9. Milbank, Jeremiah, and Grace F. Perry, *Turkey Hill Plantation*, (Self-Published, 1966. Print).

Chapter 2

10. "What Things Cost in 1942," Accessed February 20, 2014, www.tvhistory.tv.
11. "Cost of Living Info 1945," Accessed February 18, 2014, thecostofliving.com.

Chapter 3

12. "Century of Flight: Airlines and Airliners 1940-1949," Accessed April 22, 2014, www.century-of-flight.net.

Chapter 4

13. Roi Ottley, *New World A-Coming, Inside Black America (rare book)*, (Boston. Houghton Mifflin. 1943. Print).
14. "About Tennessee State University," Accessed October 25, 2012, www.tnstate.edu.

Chapter 5

15. Ibid.
16. Lynn Homan, and Thomas Reilly, *The Tuskegee Airmen, Images of America*, (Charleston, SC: Arcadia Publishing, 1998. Print), Chapters 3, 8.

Chapter 7

17. "Phoenix Arizona," Accessed June 18, 2012, en.m.wikipedia.org.
18. "Oaths of Enlistment and Oaths of Office," Accessed January 19, 2014. www.history/mil.

Chapter 8

19. The Negrito are several diverse ethnic groups who inhabit isolated parts of Austronesia. They were once considered a single population based on their physical similarities. Accessed March 16, 2020, en.m.wikipedia.org.
20. "Richard Stephen Ritchie," Accessed October 7, 2013 (update 13 April 2015), en.wikipedia.org.

Chapter 9

21. "The Philippines," Accessed November 10, 2013, www. infoplease.com/country/philippines.html.

Chapter 11

22. "United States Thunderbirds," Accessed October 9, 2013, www. thunderbirdsalumni.org.

Chapter 12

23. "China," Accessed June 5, 2014, geography.howstuffworks.com.
24. Ibid.
25. Ibid.
26. "About South Africa," Accessed June 8, 2014, www. infoplease. com/country/south-africa.html.
27. "About South Africa," Accessed June 8, 2014, www.southafric-ainfo.com.
28. "Desmond Tutu," Accessed June 8, 2014, www.biography.un/people/desmond-tutu-9512516#awesa.

Chapter 14

29. "South Korea," Accessed June 9, 2014, www.bbc.com/news/world-asia-pacific.

Chapter 20

30. "New Mexico Land of Enchantment," Accessed August 9, 2013, www.50states.com/newmexico.htm.

Chapter 22

31. "USAF 50th Anniversary Commemorative Stamps," Accessed August 5, 2013, usps.com.

Chapter 23

32. The common term *airman/airmen* describing anyone serving in the US Air Force became more widely used during General Newton's career. The long history of the world's armies and navies has made the terms *soldier* and *sailor* long-accepted monikers for anyone serving in those branches of armed forces. Military air forces, however, are relatively new; the US Air Force was officially organized in 1947. While "Airman" is the official rank of an entry-level recruit, now "airman" is used as an overall unifying reference for Air Force personnel. Ancient Roman armies and General George Patton knew themselves as "soldiers." Top Gun Naval aviators and admirals are proud to be "sailors." Newton and others knew that the Air Force needed a common noun that would draw all members of that military branch together as one entity. While it took a while for its acceptance to transition through the ranks, US Air Force men and women today have one term, one common name, that joins them together as warriors of the air: they are all *"airmen."* (This was featured in an Air Force recruiting commercial.)
33. "Order of the Sword/History of the Sword," Accessed September 20, 2013, osi.af.mil.
34. Ibid.

Appendix 1

35. "SC Legislature Honors Military Families," *The State* 26, au 2014. sec. Military News. Columbia, SC, www.thestate.com.

Appendix 2

36. "Ascend Flight Operations, Mileage Data," Accessed June 9, 2014, rockwellcollins.com.

Appendix 3

37. "General Lloyd W. 'Fig' Newton," Accessed March 26, 2011, www.af.mil/information/bios/bio.aspp?bioID=66 02.

Appendix 5

38. "Eaker Institute Colloquies: Training for the Information Age," Accessed March 26, 2011, www.afa.org/aef/pub/newton/asp.

BIBLIOGRAPHY

www.citationmachine.net
MLA version

Primary Source

The primary sources for the information in this work are personal interviews, telephone interviews, and electronic media conversations with General Lloyd Newton from July 2011 through May 2020.

Foreign Words

The English spelling "Vietnam" is used in this book versus "Viet Nam" which would require diacritics. Guidance was taken from the entry below from Hue-Tam Ho Tai of Harvard:

Hue-Tam Ho Tai, hhtai@fas.harvard.edu Wed Jun 20 02:44:45 2001 Date: Tue, 19 Jun 2001 19:51:53—0400 From: Hue Tam H. Tai <hhtai@fas.harvard.edu>

"If you are going to write Viet Nam with diacritics—that is, in Vietnamese—then it should be two words; *if you are going to leave out the diacritics, then it should be one word, English style.*"

The author (BJHH) has used the traditional spelling "Mao Tse-Tung" in the text. "Mao Zedong" is used in the Appendix.

Sources

"About South Africa." Accessed June 8, 2014. www.infoplease.com/country/south-africa.html.

"About South Africa." Accessed June 8, 2014. www.southafricainfo.com.

"About Tennessee State University." Accessed October 25, 2012. www.tnstate.edu.

"Ascend Flight Operations, Mileage Data." Accessed June 9, 2014. rockwellcollins.com.

"Century of Flight: Airlines and Airliners 1940–1949." Accessed April 22, 2014. www.century-of-flight.net.

Champlin, Kelly. "Veteran Cope Takes Flight." *Jasper County Sun*, November 9, 2011: 1, 5. Print.

"China." Accessed June 5, 2014. geography.howstuffworks.com.

"Cost of Living Info 1945." Accessed February 18, 2014. thecostof-living.com.

"Desmond Tutu." Accessed June 8, 2014. www.biography.un/people/desmond-tutu-9512516#awesa.

"Eaker Institute Colloquies: Training for the Information Age." Accessed March 26, 2011. www.afa.org/aef/pub/newton/asp.

"F-117s Arrive." Accessed February 27, 2012. www.holloman.af.mil/news/story.asp?

"Fighting the U-Boats; US Navy Tenth Fleet Fights the U-Boats." Accessed February 24, 2014. www.uboat.net/allies/ships/us_10thfleet/htm.

"General Lloyd W. Newton." Accessed March 26, 2011. www.raahistory.com/military/airforce/newton.htm.

"General Lloyd W. 'Fig' Newton." Accessed March 26, 2011. www.af.mil/information/bios/bio.aspp?bioID=6602.

Giusti, Debby. "The Legacy" poem.

"History of South Africa." Accessed June 8, 2014. un.org/cyber-schoolbus/discrim/race.b_at_print.asp.

Homan, Lynn, and Reilly, Thomas. *The Tuskegee Airmen, Images of America*. Chapters 3, 8. Charleston, SC: Arcadia Publishing, 1998. Print.

"Lloyd W. Newton." Accessed March 26, 2011. https://en.wikipedia. org/wiki/Lloyd_W._Newton.

"Lloyd W. Newton." *World Book Encyclopedia*. New York, New York: World Book, Inc., 1996. Print.

Milbank, Jeremiah, and Perry, Grace F. *Turkey Hill Plantation*: Self-Published, 1966. (rare book) Print.

"Negrito Tribe." Accessed March 16, 2020. <en.m.wikipedia.org>.

"New Mexico Land of Enchantment." Accessed August 9, 2013. www.50states.com/newmexico.htm.

"Nighthawk Celebrates 25 Years, 250K Flying Hours." Accessed March 26, 2011. www.holloman.af.mil/news/story.asp?

"Oaths of Enlistment and Oaths of Office." Accessed January 19, 2014. www.history/mil.

O'Neil, Managing Editor, Virginia. *Kids' U.S. Road Atlas*. USA: Rand McNally & Co., 1992. Print.

"Order of the Sword/History of the Sword." Accessed September 20, 2013. osi.af.mil.

Ottley, Roi. *New World A-Coming: Inside Black America. (rare book)* Boston. Houghton Mifflin, 1943. Print.

Osur, Maj. Alan M. "Black-White Relations in the U.S. Military 1940-1972." November 1,1981. Accessed September 12, 2013. http://www.airpower.maxwell.af.mil/airchronicles/aure-view/1981/nov-dec/osusr.htm.

"Phoenix Arizona." Accessed June 18, 2012. en.m.wikipedia.org.

"Plantation." Accessed August 16, 2012. en.m.wikipedia.org.

"Preserve History 1942-A Time of Attack." Accessed February 24, 2014. http://sunkenshipsobx.com/ships_1942.html.

Reedy, Jr., James R. "Coast Guard Sinking of U-352." Accessed February 24, 2014. http://diodon349.com/war/CG%20 sinks%20U352.htm.

"Richard Stephen Ritchie." Accessed October 7, 2013. en.wikipedia. org.

"SC Legislature Honors Military Families." *The State* 26 au 2014. sec. Military News. Columbia, SC. www.thestate.com.

Saunders, Richard M. *Carolina Quest.* Chapter 7. Toronto Canada and Columbia, SC: University of Toronto Press and University of South Carolina Press, 1951. Print.

Sawyer Ashton, Patricia, and Ray E. Ashton Jr. *The Gopher Tortoise, A Life History.* Sarasota, FL: Pineapple Press, Inc., 2004. Print.

"South Carolina Aviation Hall of Fame." Accessed April 7, 2012. www.sconline.com/hall-of-fame.

"South Korea." Accessed June 9, 2014. www.bbc.com/news/world-asia-pacific.

The Armed Forces Officer. Chapters VIII, IX, X. Washington, DC: U. S. Government Printing Office, 1950. Print.

"The Geography of South Africa." Accessed June 8, 2014. www.geography.about.com/od/southafricamaps.

"The Philippines." Accessed July 15, 2012. www.ephillipine.com.

"The Philippines." Accessed November 10, 2013. www.infoplease.com/country/philippines.html.

"The Town of Ridgeland, South Carolina." Accessed March 26, 2011. www.ridgelandsc.gov.

"Thunderbird's First African American Pilot Becomes Four-Star General." Accessed March 6, 2011. www.scaaonline.com/hall-of-fam/HoF%20Pages/Newton%20Lloyd.htm.

"Timeline of Chinese History" Accessed June 8, 2014. https://en.wikipedia.org/wiki/Timeline_of_Chinese_history.

"Top News Stories from 1942–2000." Accessed June 16, 2014. infoplease.com.

"Tuskegee Airmen." Accessed May 14, 2013. www.tuskegeeairmen.org.

"USAF 50th Anniversary Commemorative Stamps." Accessed August 5, 2013. usps.com.

"United States Thunderbirds." Accessed October 9, 2013. www.thunderbirdsalumni.org.

"What Things Cost in 1942." Accessed February 20, 2014. www.tvhistory.tv.

ABOUT THE AUTHORS

Lloyd Newton, an accomplished Air Force officer and pilot, was born in a small, segregated town in South Carolina during WWII. He learned early on from his parents that education and hard work are important factors for success and achieving dreams. From a very early age, Newton had an intense desire to serve in the US military. While working on his family's small farm, he often saw military and civilian airplanes flying overhead, but as an African-American living in the South, he could not imagine piloting an aircraft. That, however, would change. Newton had his first flight in the spring of 1962 during his freshman year at Tennessee State University where he studied aviation and was a member of the Air Force Reserve Officer Training Corps (AFROTC).

Upon graduation, he was commissioned a 2nd Lieutenant and entered Air Force pilot training in June 1966. He pinned on his silver wings in June 1967. Newton departed for the war in Vietnam on April 4, 1968, the day Dr. Martin Luther King Jr. was shot and killed. He spent a year in Vietnam where he flew the F-4 Phantom on a total of 269 combat missions, 79 over North Vietnam.

Newton dreamed of flying with the US Air Force Demonstration Team, "The Thunderbirds." He was selected for the team in 1974 after three attempts as the *first* African-American Thunderbird pilot.

He progressed from plowing the fields of a small South Carolina farm to some of the highest levels of command in the US Air Force. He flew more than 4,000 hours in various military aircraft including the T-38 Talon, F-4 Phantom, F-15 Eagle, F-16 Falcon, and F-117 Stealth Fighter. He retired from the USAF in June 2000 as a four-star General.

A committed leader throughout his life, Newton emphasizes to others that their destiny is not determined by their circumstances but by the decisions they make!

B. J. Harvey Hill is a career elementary educator, having taught in the public, private, home-schooling, and teacher-training sectors. During the second half of her career her concentration was science, teaming with NASA, National Science Foundation, University of South Florida graduate science researchers and the beginning of the STEM movement. A magna cum laude graduate of the University of Cincinnati, she did post graduate work at University of South Florida and St. Leo's University, specializing in elementary science and non-fiction writing.

She is a South Carolina master naturalist; loving and respecting all of nature. As an aviation enthusiast and pilot, she has been a 22-year multi-area participant at the Sun 'n Fun annual general aviation event whose mission is: "To engage, educate, and accelerate the next generation of aviation professionals."

This native of Tennessee has lived many places, "blooming where she's planted" along the way. Faith and family have always been the most important parts of life, spiced with wonderful friendships along the way.

Helping others rise to their potential is one of her ongoing goals. By introducing young people to contemporary nonfiction, especially biographies of living mentors, the stories of people making a difference throughout the world can inspire and positively influence the reader's life choices.

When Hill met General Newton, they found common interests in aviation and youth education. They both felt it was time for Newton's story to be told. Now this author wants to encourage each reader to find that story, as yet untold, to capture themselves!

CPSIA information can be obtained
at www.ICGtesting.com
Printed in the USA
FSHW021340140221